T0158470

"Write Nothing about Politics"

*Last passport photo of Hans Bernd
von Haeften, July 1944*

"Write Nothing about Politics"

A PORTRAIT OF HANS BERND VON HAEFTEN

By Barbara von Haeften

Translated by Julie M. Winter

Michigan State University Press | *East Lansing*

♾ The paper used in this publication meets the minimum requirements
of ANSI/NISO Z39.48-1992 (R 1997) (Permanence of Paper).

MICHIGAN STATE UNIVERSITY PRESS
East Lansing, Michigan 48823-5245

Printed and bound in the United States of America.

27 26 25 24 23 22 21 20 19 18   1 2 3 4 5 6 7 8 9 10

LIBRARY OF CONGRESS CATALOGING-IN-PUBLICATION DATA
names: Haeften, Barbara von, 1908– author.
Title: "Write nothing about politics": a Portrait of Hans Bernd von Haeften
/ Barbara von Haeften ; translated by Julie M. Winter.
Other titles: Nichts Schriftliches von Politik. English
Description: East Lansing: Michigan State University Press, 2018.
| "Nichts Schriftliches von Politik. Hans Bernd von Haeften: Ein Lebensbericht
© 1997 by Barbara von Haeften; foreword © 2018 Arnold Steinhardt;
English translation and translator's introduction © 2018 Julie M. Winter."
| Includes bibliographical references.
Identifiers: LCCN 2017025952| ISBN 9781611862799 (pbk.: alk. paper)
| ISBN 9781609175597 (pdf) | ISBN 9781628953275 (epub)
| ISBN 9781628963274 (kindle)
Subjects: LCSH: Haeften, Hans Bernd von, 1905-1944. | Anti-Nazi movement—
Germany—Biography. | Germany—Politics and government—1933-1945.
Classification: LCC DD256.3 .H1813 2018 | DDC 943.086092 [B]—dc23
LC record available at https://lccn.loc.gov/2017025952

Book design by Charlie Sharp, Sharp Des!gns, East Lansing, MI
Cover design by Shaun Allshouse, www.shaunallshouse.com

Michigan State University Press is a member of the Green Press
Initiative and is committed to developing and encouraging
ecologically responsible publishing practices. For more information
about the Green Press Initiative and the use of recycled paper
in book publishing, please visit *www.greenpressinitiative.org.*

Visit Michigan State University Press at *www.msupress.org*

Contents

Foreword

Arnold Steinhardt

Sometime towards the end of World War II, my father summoned me, age seven, to the short wave radio he was listening to and said purposefully, "You won't understand what this madman, Adolf Hitler, is saying in German, but I want you to hear his voice and remember it forever."

When the disastrous war was finally over, Hitler dead, and the Nazis vanquished, father learned that almost all of his relatives had perished in Auschwitz. With this background as an American Jew fortunate enough to grow up in the safety of the far away United States while war raged in Europe, I entered adult life probably viewing the German-speaking people as most Jews did. To my mind, they were all criminals and murderers, especially as I listened to dad break down in tears as he attempted to tell us about his family whom he would never see again.

This stark view of Germans began to change when I fell in love with and then married a German woman, Dorothea von Haeften. I soon learned through her mother, Barbara von Haeften, whom I came to love dearly and with whom I had a special bond, that while there were indeed many criminals, murderers, and deeply misguided people responsible for the calamitous war, others among their ranks detested and resisted the Nazis. In particular, there were men and women deeply disturbed with the Nazi's persecution and extermination of the Jewish people. Dorothea's parents, Barbara and Hans Bernd von Haeften, were such people.

In *"Write Nothing about Politics,"* Barbara von Haeften brings to life her husband's deeply held religious convictions and his profound opposition to killing another human being, even Adolph Hitler. Von Haeften relates how her husband slowly came to believe that the head must be cut off for the snake to die, that Hitler must be eliminated if a new Germany would have any future. She describes in heart stopping detail how Hans von Haeften and many like-minded people envisioned a German future after the collapse of the Third Reich, how they secretly planned, under constant threat of exposure, the assassination attempt, and how the plot tragically failed. Hans and Barbara von Haeften left nothing written down about politics for fear of ever-suspicious censors.

More or less at the same time that dad and I listened to Adolf Hitler on the shortwave radio, Hans Bernd von Haeften stood before a judge at the People's Court in Germany, about to be condemned to death for his role in the assassination attempt. My father had the luxury of branding Hitler a monster without consequence in the safety of the United States, while Hans Bernd von Haeften paid with his life for his actions, stating at his trial with unimaginable courage that Hitler was the embodiment of evil.

Von Haeften's life is both inspiring and heart breaking to contemplate. In his widow Barbara's compelling recounting of their time together, there lurks a literally unmentioned but nonetheless powerful question for me and any other reader to answer. What kind of a German would I have been during the war—a rabid Nazi, an unquestioning follower, or a Hans Bernd von Haeften?

I find no easy answer to this question.

Translator's Introduction

BARBARA VON HAEFTEN WAS BORN IN DUISBURG, GERMANY, in 1908, and grew up in Heidelberg and Berlin as the daughter of Julius and Adda Curtius. Her father was politically active in the government of the Weimar Republic and became the Minister of Economics and later Minister of Foreign Affairs. In 1930 Barbara married Hans Bernd von Haeften, born in Berlin in 1905, who studied law and entered diplomatic service, eventually becoming a legation counselor at the Ministry of Culture. His parents were Hans von Haeften, an army officer and later head of the Reich Archive, and Agnes von Brauchitsch, sister of Walther von Brauchitsch, the Commander-in-Chief of the German Army from 1938–1941.

"*Nichts Schriftliches von Politik.*" *Hans Bernd von Haeften: Ein Lebensbericht* (1997), translated here, is Barbara von Haeften's only published work. After 1945, she lived in Lake Constance and Heidelberg, and in 1975 with her daughter near Munich until her death in 2006.

Barbara von Haeften's work, part memoir and part biography, chronologically reconstructs her husband Hans's life based on her recollection of events and on numerous letters to and from him.

Barbara's main motivation for writing this memoir was to depict her husband as the politically active person that he was, an important element of his life and work that she felt had not sufficiently come to light. One reason for this was that Hans had rarely written about politics in his letters because he knew that the Gestapo had begun surveillance of him and his activities early on; he therefore had to be extremely careful not to incriminate himself, his family, and the friends he helped and was politically involved with.

The broad scope of Hans's political activities do become apparent in this narrative: Barbara and Hans both opposed and took actions against the Nazi regime as soon as it came into power. Hans helped Jewish friends escape from Germany beginning as early as 1933, and the couple became members of the Confessing Church that fought Nazi control of the churches in the early phase of the protest movement. In spite of his government position, Hans refused to become a member of the Nazi party, and while working abroad he became involved with ethnic German groups, whose members had become Hitler supporters, in order to try to dissuade them from National Socialism.

More and more distressed by Hitler's persecution of the Jews, Hans became active in the Kreisau Circle resistance group in the early 1940s and was ultimately closely connected to the July 20, 1944, plot to assassinate Hitler. In fact, his brother, Werner von Haeften, was Claus von Stauffenberg's aide and helped von Stauffenberg carry out the assassination attempt. Both Werner von Haeften and Claus von Stauffenberg were executed on the day of the failed coup. Hans was arrested shortly afterwards and hanged on August 15, 1944. Barbara was also arrested on July 25, 1944, and was not allowed to take her newborn baby, her fifth child, to prison with her. She was released on September 30, 1944.

The Kreisau Circle was a loosely organized group of resisters whose participants came from a broad spectrum of German society. Politicians, clergy, trade-union leaders, government officials, and members of the military, among others, belonged to the group whose primary goal was to plan for a new government after the fall of Hitler. The Gestapo named the group after the estate of Helmuth James Count von Moltke, one of the co-founders of the Circle, along with Peter Yorck Count von Wartenburg. Members of the inner circle met at the Moltke estate in Silesia on three separate occasions, and they also met frequently in Berlin, often at Marion and Peter Yorck's apartment.

Firmly grounded in his Christian faith, Hans could not initially support the murder of Hitler. However, he changed his mind and came to support the assassination plan. Barbara's memoir reveals Hans's struggle to come to terms with the dictates of his conscience, and it is illuminating to follow his increasing involvement in resistance to an evil regime. Hans' particular struggle was rooted in the fact that he, as a government official, was part of a system that murdered and destroyed. In addition, he was not a military man, and he did not feel that courage came easily to him. Nevertheless, he was able to take part in action that sought to bring down the Nazis and that cost him his life. In the end, it was his love for his fellow human beings and his strong Christian faith that helped him do what he knew was right.

Historical scholarship has given us detailed information about the plans, goals, membership, and activities of the Kreisau Circle, and an English translation of a first-person account is an important addition to the material already available. Memoirs such as Barbara's make real what daily life in a totalitarian regime was like and what it took in terms of personality, stamina, and determination to rebel in such a system. We also come to know a truly exceptional person—Hans von Haeften—who stands out among his contemporaries due to his great humanity, intelligence, compassion, Christian faith, and courage. This portrait of Hans's very personal struggle as a participant in the Resistance is a testament to Barbara's profound love and admiration for her husband.

Barbara does not give us details about herself, other than in the context of her husband's activities or in matters of family arrangements due to his change of positions in the government. Nevertheless, a picture also emerges of her—and one is struck by her unconditional support for his actions, her strong Christian faith, and her optimistic personality. It becomes clear that her role in the Resistance was as important as his.

Some personal names that Barbara uses in the memoir may cause confusion. "Mütt" is a term of endearment that the family used for Barbara's mother, Adda Curtius, and "Omaletti" refers to Barbara's mother-in-law, Agnes von Haeften. She mentions the names of many people the von Haeftens knew and worked with; the context of the passages will give the reader a general idea of their roles.

I would like to thank Barbara's family for reading the translation, offering many helpful suggestions concerning wording and accuracy, and supplying the English version of Hans's farewell letter, included at the end of Barbara's narrative. I hope that our collective efforts will lead to a broader awareness of the lives and sacrifices of those who dared to resist the Nazi terror state.

"Write Nothing about Politics"

N ALL THE YEARS SINCE JULY 20, 1944, MUCH HAS BEEN PUB-
lished about the German Resistance against Hitler. But nowhere
does my husband, Hans Bernd von Haeften, clearly appear as the
politically active person he was. For this reason, I am now trying
to collect and record as much as possible by Hans and about him.
Due to constant surveillance by the Gestapo from 1936 on, he left
no writings behind except some personal letters. Ever since the
first time our house was in danger of being searched in 1933, we had
made it a rule that nothing about politics should appear in our letters. We were, by the way, seldom apart during our fourteen years
of marriage and therefore rarely needed to write to each other.

"WHEN I TRIED TO IMAGINE WHAT I MIGHT WRITE, I WAS
shocked by how difficult it was," wrote Hans's best friend Günther
Hill in 1946, in regard to Ricarda Huch's request to send material
for her planned book. In spite of his misgivings, I feel that Günther's picture of Hans comes close to life:

> I have so many memories of him, most of them quite clear.
> . . . It was nothing specific, no specific talents, characteris-
> tics, abilities or accomplishments—it was the irresistible
> charm of his whole personality, his whole demeanor. It was
> not his intellect, his character, his ability to take things in,
> or his ideas, but rather a remarkable and very rare harmony
> in which these qualities were united in him, a harmony that
> was expressed not in words or thoughts, but often more
> profoundly and clearly in a gesture, a smile or a movement.

We read and worked together, tried to understand ourselves and God and the world. Much of what we took very seriously then appears to me to be false and outdated today. What remains is the man I can still picture as so alive, as though I had just seen him yesterday, so clearly that I will never believe that he is no longer here.

In order to give a clearer picture of Hans, I can also offer an observation made by my mother, preserved in a letter from Pastor Maas dated January 1, 1948: "Yesterday morning your mother described him to me movingly, and told me what a light emanated from him when he so much as stepped into a room, and how a sense of clear thinking and emotional depth came over the people he met. That is the greatest thing that can be said about a man and also the most enduring."

In addition, I'll quote from a letter I wrote in 1946 to Ricarda Huch, who asked me to write about Hans:

You ask whether my husband also had that radiant look that was definitely so characteristic of his brother Werner. I think that the carefree happiness that radiated from Werner, as well as his joyful laughter, was not characteristic of my husband. In my opinion, his eyes reflected more his kindness, intelligence, and integrity. . . . It was amazing how he could concentrate on the most difficult mental work, as well as on pleasant children's games and relaxing vacations, which we took both with and without our dear children. I would love to show you a few pictures where his delightful relationship to our children can be seen. . . . His delicate health and his sensitive soul were closely connected. Because of that he had much to fight and much to endure. Body and soul suffered in the same

amount under the 'horrors of devastation.' I do not need
to write about his devoutness and increasing grounded-
ness in prayer, since all the documents I am sending,
especially his goodbye letter, give the best evidence of
these. He always had his confirmation text nearby where
he could see it:

Be watchful, stand firm in the faith,
Be manly and be strong. (1 Corinthians 16:13)

As a child he had his brother paint the text in Greek,
in white letters on a red background with a blue border.
The relationship between the two brothers was simply
beautiful. They completed each other in many respects.
You should especially know about their readiness to help
all those in distress, and of their ability to lift people's
spirits. They were a wonderful support to their mother
after the death of their father. Werner's innate cheerful-
ness comforted her, whereas my husband helped with his
deep compassion and spiritual wisdom. But the brothers
also comforted and helped those who were not so close
to the family, and they bravely supported many who were
politically persecuted with advice and direct action. Using
strict self-discipline, my husband had trained himself since
adolescence to practice remarkable civil courage, while his
brother most likely was able to achieve this virtue with less
difficulty. In this, as in all the chivalrous virtues, they had
a shining example in their father.

I WOULD NOW LIKE TO GIVE SOME IMPORTANT DATES FROM
Hans's life and describe his political development. The First World
War definitely played a large role in the development of the three

children. Elisabeth, known as "Liet," was born in December 1903, Hans Bernd in December 1905, and Werner in October 1908. Their mother Agnes, née von Brauchitsch, was a very sensitive and introverted person, who tended to be melancholy, but who was also very assertive. She had definite likes and dislikes. Their father liked to describe a remarkable experience: As the head of the Reich Archives, he and their mother were invited to the large reception at the Reich President's on May 1, 1933. When Hitler, as Reich Chancellor, greeted them, their mother's expression was so unwelcoming that Hitler hesitated for a moment to extend her his hand. Their father, on the other hand, had an engaging personality. Meinecke described him in this way: "Everyone who came into contact with him was, first of all, struck by his intellect, his idealism, and his imagination, which was always active and yet critically held in check. Then they would notice an unusual grace in his nature, which flowed from the depths of his character and was free of all vanity." Ludendorff praised him for having "a capacity for work fueled by his idealism," and the "gift of supporting and carrying his co-workers along." He was an active officer, called up early (1902–1907) to the Military Academy and appointed to the General Staff of the Eastern Commander-in-Chief beginning in December 1914. As the adjutant of Hindenburg and Ludendorff, he was immediately pulled into the crisis of the two-front war. After great losses in the West, at the Battle of the Marne, Hindenburg and Ludendorff wanted to focus the war effort on the East. Father Haeften was sent to the Kaiser with a letter containing these plans. In spite of the outraged objections of the Kaiser, Father Haeften also personally declared his support for this oppositional demand. At this the Kaiser—enraged—tore the national emblem from his uniform and the sword from his side, locked him into the nearest room, and had him quickly put before a court-martial. He received a disciplinary transfer to Brussels, without decorations or medals.

Father Haeften described this scene now and again in the family circle with great pleasure. The official version was merely that "he fell for some months in disgrace." Much later, after the death of their father, Hans Bernd wanted to publish a chapter from his father's memoirs "The Crisis of the Two-Front War," somewhat modified, as a warning to Hitler against attacking Russia. But this project immediately failed to pass censorship and was never published.

By the summer of 1916, Father Haeften had been transferred by Falkenhayn, the head of the General Staff, to the military's news department in the Foreign Office, and he remained there until the end of the war. He assembled a staff of talented men, and with his balanced objectivity, he was able to function as a mediator in difficult domestic situations. One of his closest co-workers was Kurt Hahn, whom he brought into his department as an English editor from the central bureau of the Foreign Office, in spite of official protests about Hahn's critical reporting. He worked closely with Hahn until the end of the war.

I quote Prince Max von Baden, who wrote the following about Hans's father:

> I heard from Haeften's co-workers that it was not always easy to keep up with his pace. They said he was not easily annoyed, but he was occasionally irate. Indiscretion and petty vanity could make him furious. At times chairs were said to hit the walls. But there was not a person in the whole place who would not have gone through fire for him. (Prinz Max von Baden, *Erinnerungen und Dokumente* [Stuttgart: Deutsche Verlagsanstalt, 1927], 81)

During the years 1916–1918, Kurt Hahn was also a guest of the Haeften family. As an educator, he recognized Hans Bernd's political interests and talent and advised his parents to orient Hans's education toward diplomatic service, as well as to organize his study abroad in England. And so, early on, they looked for a student exchange for him.

While growing up, Hans actively experienced the excitement of the war and the capitulation and abdication of the Kaiser, as well as the difficult rebuilding of the parliamentary republic. With his siblings and friends he had dug trenches in the family garden—to the point of over-exertion, so much so that his doctor ordered him not to participate in sports at school. At around twelve years of age he staged parliamentary sessions with his friends, which included exciting debates and speeches in front of the entire assembly.

As a young man, Hans mentioned with pride that his ancestors belonged to the "Watergeuzen." Along with William of Orange, they had fought Spanish oppression and the Inquisition in the sixteenth century and ultimately fought to secure the Netherlands' independence from Spain. When Hans's brother Werner was executed by gunfire after the failed assassination attempt of Hitler on July 20, 1944, he cried out "I die for freedom!" as he threw himself in front of Stauffenberg. With his courageous behavior while serving in a responsible political position, their father had undoubtedly set the standard for the death-defying commitment of the two sons against Hitler's murderous antisemitism and megalomania.

In 1921, Liet and Hans were confirmed in Berlin-Grunewald together with Dietrich Bonhoeffer and his twin sister. Although they were usually not in the same area, Hans and Dietrich remained closely aligned from that time until their deaths in 1944 and 1945 in their brave opposition to Hitler and National Socialism, supported by their Christian faith. Bonhoeffer began to form a separate ecumenical office of the Confessing Church in 1935 and in a letter to President Koch he named those who were "desired for closer collaboration," among others "Legation Secretary H.v.

Haeften—Dahlem, very interested in the matter and prepared to give a lot of time to it, completely with us" (June 4, 1935, as quoted in Bonhoeffer, *Gesammelte Schriften,* edited by Eberhard Bethge [München: Kaiser, 1958–1974]). When Bonhoeffer traveled to Stockholm in 1942, he received information from Hans during an unobserved "walk" about the state of things in the Kreisau Friends' Circle in order to pass it on to the English, especially Churchill, through the Bishop of Chichester. And after his return they also met "by chance" in Podbielskiallee Station in order to exchange news. In the winter of 1943, shortly before Bonhoeffer's arrest, Hans met him once more in secret.

In their final school years, a friendship began between Hans and Günther Hill (at that time spelled "Hell"), which "had a decisive influence on my life," as Günther wrote in 1946 in the letter cited above. It was also decisive for Hans in many ways. For example, Günther was a Jew, which certainly contributed to Hans's political awareness and early resistance to Hitler. Already in 1933 Günther had to quit his classical philology studies at the university. Kurt Hahn, the friend and co-worker of Father Haeften's during the war and revolutionary time, was also a Jew. He was arrested in March of 1933 in Salem and had to emigrate. At the beginning of the 1930s, Hahn visited us several times in Berlin because he hoped to find ways with Hans to help make the older generation of politicians aware of the danger lurking in Hitler, and to convince them that they must never allow him to come into power.

Hans had collected drafts for warnings, speeches, and brochures in a file and had written on the cover:

The time will come
When the nobles will conspire
And the miserable wretches will fall into their nets.
[reversed quote from the end of Goethe's *Götz von Berlichingen*]

In 1935 we left the file for safety reasons in Copenhagen, but the Friends burned it when the Nazis marched in.

IN THE SPRING OF 1924 HANS COMPLETED HIS EXAMS AT THE classically oriented Bismarck Secondary School. The excellent teachers at this school, some of whom he kept in touch with, strongly influenced his intellectual development. At his father's wish, following his schooling, Hans had to go for at least half a year into the Reichswehr, which was actually forbidden at the end of the First World War and for that reason called the "Black Reichswehr." Father Haeften was at that time still of the opinion that "boys should be toughened up." Later with Werner he was less severe. For Hans, the time in the military was not an enjoyable experience. He was, as he often said later, "a born civilian." He soon contracted a bad intestinal illness, the "red runs," which recurred and left him with an intestinal weakness.

In the fall of 1924 Hans began to study law in Berlin, continued his studies for a year in Munich, and then went back to Berlin. Smend, Werner Jaeger, Regenbogen, Erich Kaufmann, and Siegmund-Schultze are all names from that time that I often heard. I also received poems from Munich, for in March of 1925 Hans and I had caught each other's eye (he was nineteen years old, and I was sixteen), and from then on we remained close, even though we were seldom together—and never by ourselves. How different from nowadays! Not until the time of Hans's licensing exams did it come to the defining exchange of letters, and on March 27, 1928, we were engaged.

Hans was an exchange student in England from 1928–1929 at Trinity College in Cambridge. During this year he gained a great deal of experience with people and politics. But it was not an easy time; in particular, he had trouble with the language at the beginning, for at that time English was not taught in classical secondary schools. Furthermore, in the first semester his lodgings were quite primitive and had no heat. In addition, the English pies and other college foods didn't agree with him. But no one in Cambridge knew about all these difficulties; only I knew from his letters. From the start he was able to meet his tutor's demanding requirements—weekly essays, which were then discussed with the tutor. Right away he had the topic: "About the Value of the Reinsurance Treaty," about which he commented to me in a letter: "I knew nothing about this topic, and since the 'Reinsurance Treaty' probably inaugurated the most intelligent politics that Bismarck ever carried out, but at the same time the most entangled and difficult to understand, I became completely involved with learning about it and then—of course, only with the help of an Englishman—translating the whole thing, which is incredibly difficult due to the technical terms. In addition, I had my lectures to attend and rowing every day, which makes me very tired"—and which his Berlin doctor had forbidden. The lectures were about constitutional history and contemporary English political theory: "Problems of Government Formation," "Constitutional History 1485," "English Economic History," "General Theory of the State in Modern Times." Immediately after that he wrote an essay "The Relation between Cabinet and House of Commons in England, Legally and Actually" then "The English Church as a Halfway House between Rome and Geneva"—"the most difficult part of church history," Hans commented to me.

At Easter in 1929, Hans was able to spend a worthwhile vacation in London and also to take part in a study week at the "Students' Settlement Union," similar to the "Social Work Community of Berlin-Ost" led by Siegmund-Schultze. Hans regarded Siegmund-Schultze highly ever since he had taken part, with his sister Liet, in activities led by him in Berlin-Ost. Both kept in contact, on a personal and political level, with the same goal in mind:

to strengthen the opposition to Hitler. In 1939 Sigmund-Schultze visited us in Bucharest, and later in Berlin Hans used every opportunity he had to visit him in Switzerland. As a Social Democrat, Siegmund-Schultze had already had to emigrate there in 1933.

During his last months in Cambridge, Hans worked in the area of international law. In the Debating Club he had to give a lecture about the Versailles Treaty; Churchill sat in the audience.

From January 1, 1930, until the beginning of August, Hans was an office assistant at the German consulate in Geneva. There he learned about various aspects of office life. However, the work was all in German and barely left him time to learn French. I quote from his letters to me:

> The work in the consulate is quite varied, part pure consulate work, that is, economic matters, legal matters, general support, gathering information and advice concerning just about everything. Another part of it concerns League of Nations work, mediating between the League of Nations and the Foreign Office, gathering information (for me a gradual training in thousands of contracts, conventions and statutes), participation in committee meetings, and so on. And part of it is pure political work, daily press readings and press conferences, and so on. Above all, I must write reports, reports, and more reports on all matters. Social duties—which are a waste of time—are some of my main activities; unfortunately, there is no French or Geneva circle at all. The people of Geneva, very exclusive anyway, don't want to have anything to do with Germans, even the press is sometimes inflammatory. By the way, the thing that is most unpleasantly evident here and makes one have many second thoughts is the shocking atmosphere of

intrigue among all those who are somehow connected to the Foreign Office. This includes the German section of the International Employment Office, the German section of the League of Nations, and the German consulate. They all conspire against one another and among themselves; each one thinks only of his nice little position, his career, and the possibility of one-upping his rival, bringing him into disrepute. Bow and scrape, no consistent management, a totally toxic atmosphere. At any rate, if you don't have a huge amount of money or a thousand little protections and connections, and if you don't cleverly plot and scheme, then you should not go into this kind of work in the first place.

In August his consular service was over.

On September 2, 1930, we were married. Hans had planned our honeymoon trip well—we went to Dresden, Prague, Salzburg, Kärnten, and Vienna, all unknown to me until that point.

We now lived in Berlin-Schmargendorf, and Hans became secretary of the Stresemann Foundation and the Society for Study in Eastern Europe, and, in addition, the leader of the newly founded circle of Friends of the College for Politics under Professor Jaeckh.

From January 12–15, 1931, Hans took part in an international disarmament conference in Oxford. There he successfully joined a debate. "'I had to put up a gallant fight,' as Admiral Richmond put it today," Hans wrote in a letter to me. He came to the attention of Secretary of State von Simson, who then let it be known in the Foreign Office that Hans should be encouraged to take the qualifying examination. Since it was very difficult for a long time to get accepted into the Foreign Office, Hans had decided to train as a legal assessor. In April of that year he accompanied Professor Erich Kaufmann to the International Court in The Hague and successfully assisted him in difficult negotiations with the Poles.

On July 19, 1931, our first child, Johan Adam, was born. We called him Jan.

In the fall of 1932, Hans was requested by the Foreign Office to take the qualifying examination on April 1, 1933, with the hint that they wanted to select him for employment from the group of applicants that had grown considerably in number. After a short preparation in Paris—mainly to practice the language—Hans passed the test and began his training as an attaché on May 1, 1933, in the Foreign Office.

The training course in the Foreign Office was interrupted in the fall, and the attachés were sent by the Nazi regime into a quickly militarized work camp. Hans and a colleague were sent to East Prussia, where swamps were being drained in the Memel area. Hans had unexpectedly good relations there with the younger unemployed communists from the Ruhr area, and he instructed them in political matters. He gave a lecture on "European Pacts and State Treaties" and wrote to me about it in September 1933:

> The young men were rather taken with it and asked excellent questions. In a down-to-earth manner I gave them facts which were probably new to them and interested them all the more, since they are thoroughly fed up with the empty gibberish of election speeches. They had the feeling that they were finally hearing what is really happening. It is interesting that they were so thankful for *that*. The leader of the camp skipped the lecture, but I am satisfied that I found resonance with the fellows.

The last three days had been "very demanding, because I must constantly talk about something in the evenings—The Battle of the Marne or otherwise something about the war, politics, personal experiences and so on. They want to use the days in order to learn as much as possible." Later he wrote: "Everything again went very well, including the second lecture about security and disarmament."

Our friend Schorsch Maier, an assistant professor in Roman law, had to go to a similar work camp. He enlightened his colleagues there about the essence of the legal state. As he was leaving the camp in the fall of 1933, he was suddenly thrown into a truck and taken to the concentration camp Sachsenhausen, where he disappeared. He was the first of our friends to undergo such a fate. Hans went to great lengths for him and was able to free him with the help of an attorney in the spring of 1934, something that was still possible at that time. At the baptism of our second son Dirk in March by Martin Niemöller, we missed Schorsch, as godfather, terribly.

BY 1931 BONHOEFFER HAD ALREADY INTRODUCED HANS TO Niemöller. They quickly became friends; they especially agreed on politics and the church struggle. Naturally, we belonged to the Confessing Church from the very start. I still have our red membership cards, numbers 456 and 457, dated September 26, 1934, from the Lutheran parish in Dahlem. On the back is printed:

> The Confessing Church is the union of all those who recognize the holy writings of the Old and New Testaments, according to the interpretation of the reformation faiths, as the only basis of the church and its proclamation. The members of the Confessing Church are called by the Gospel. For that reason we desire to keep God's word and the table of the Lord and lead a Christian life. We desire to pray and work for a renewal of the church from the word and the spirit of God. We know we are duty bound to resolutely

fight against every forgery of the Gospel and against all use of force and coercion of conscience in the church.

On July 26, 1933, Hans wrote to me: "Dahlem is in fact the only Berlin community with a sixty percent majority on the list 'Gospel and Church.' And yet, in Grunewald, Nikolassee, Wannsee, Zehlendorf, etc. the conditions are at least as favorable. One sees how crucial the pastor is." In our case, Niemöller. Our friendship with the Niemöllers also continued despite our stays abroad. In the summer of 1935 we even traveled together through the Black Forest, and we also visited the Niemöllers in Heiden in Switzerland. And at the beginning of the 1940s, when Niemöller was imprisoned in a concentration camp, his wife was sometimes with us in the evening in Dahlem; usually she was dead tired, and it was difficult for her to stay awake.

On January 5, 1934, our second son Dirk was born. Hans was transferred on April 1, 1934, to the embassy in Copenhagen, while I waited with our two small sons in Dahlem at my parents' until Hans found us an apartment. As an attaché, he was soon offered preferential admittance into the NSDAP, even though they were actually not taking any more members. He refused, which earned him the first black mark in his personal file. In addition, there was his critical memo to the Foreign Office—for although the ambassador had requested an "older attaché with a wife to keep his wife company," neither the moving costs nor the travel tickets were included for a wife with two sons and the necessary household help. Until then, no married attachés had come up in the budget. In any case, the budget rules were changed and later attachés profited from Hans's memo. In a letter dated May 1934 he wrote: "The office duties here can, of course, not be compared to those in Berlin: it is much, much more unpleasant. But that's just the way it is." There were also frequent diplomatic parties and other social activities: "All in all, I believe, it is in our interest to spend only eight months here and then go back to Berlin. If I don't have to quit Foreign Service, that is. The night life ruins everyone in the long run: one's spirit can only stand the unpleasant socializing for a limited time."

In any case, Hans soon made contact with Pastor Görnandt, who because of his "non-Aryan" wife was no longer acceptable to his lively church in Potsdam. It became a very stimulating friendship for us. We visited his "Luther Lessons" and got used to regular church going—not just as a way to oppose the German Christians.

IN APRIL 1935 HANS CAME BACK TO THE FOREIGN OFFICE IN Berlin. Dietrich Bonhoeffer and his friend Hildebrandt were often our lunch guests. There were intense conversations about church and politics. We were happy to be in Dahlem again, the place where everything was happening, in the Niemöller community. But by the fall Hans was transferred to Vienna as the cultural attaché under Ambassador von Papen. In spite of the distance, Hans continued to closely follow the disputes in the church struggle in Germany. The struggle quickly intensified after the appointment of Kerrl as the minister for religious matters, and with the formation of church committees which threatened to split the Confessing Church. Hans replied to my very concerned report from Dahlem on January 18, 1936:

> Concerning church matters, the most important thing is clarity, and that must be achieved by asking questions that cannot be evaded. It would probably be best if Dietrich [Bonhoeffer] and Kurt [Scharf] would get together, and then give Martin [Niemöller] the decision at the final edit. Hopefully the others will subsequently notice

afterwards—as usual—that Niemöller is on the right path and will join him again. . . . Strange, the way religious questions take center stage everywhere. I was at Muff's [the military attaché at the German embassy] for dinner, with Nostitz and others. Things were quite lively. The women were once again on my side during the heated debates (letter dated January 9, 1936).

In turn, I was able to report, almost at the same time, from the Rhineland to Hans about my Grandmother Carp:

She is a faithful member of the Confessing Church and would like to learn more about the events there. Yesterday I read a portion of the Steglitz Synod decree to her, which in regard to baptism interested her a lot. . . . Wolfgang also talked about this topic on his own yesterday and said that according to his Dutch newspaper, hard times were coming and, he feared, especially hard times for our Martin [Niemöller].

So it was quite natural for Hans to also enter into a conversation with Herbert Krimm in Vienna (vicar at the Dorothee Church at that time). He told him about the events in the church struggle, about which Krimm knew hardly anything up to that point. Hans wrote about the New Year's Eve and New Year sermons in the Dorothee Church: "Both sermons were quite good, but of course the atmosphere of the great conflict and its secular resolution is missing, the atmosphere that, in Dahlem, penetrates every sermon as the focus of the struggle." Hans and Krimm enjoyed lively conversations about theological questions, and an enduring friendship developed that continued later in letters. During the Vienna time Krimm, still unmarried, was often our guest, even on trips with the children to the Lainz Zoological Garden, the Viennese Forest, and on swimming excursions.

Through Krimm, Hans became acquainted with the Evangelical Brotherhood of St. Michael and with their efforts to renew the church service. He enjoyed participating in the St. Michael's celebration in October 1935 in Marburg and meeting some of the brothers there. But he was often critical, and he admonished, in later letters to Krimm, that "part of the renewal of the genuine life of the church is that the church publicly proclaims Christ . . . that it—as all the apostles did—gives witness and proclaims the word among the people . . . that it remains the church and does not allow itself to deteriorate into a sect or a conventicle or a museum." In Berlin during the years 1941–1943, Hans often participated as a guest in services and discussions with the Brothers of St. Michael, but he never became a member. "Somehow they are too narrow for me," was his comment to me about it, after he had rejected the membership offered to him in the fall of 1943.

As the cultural attaché in Vienna, Hans soon had connections to the Ministry of Culture. There he found a friend in Under-Secretary Wilhelm Wolf, with whom he could discuss political, intellectual, and spiritual matters. In 1938 Wolf was the Secretary of State for several weeks, but he was quickly swept out of the way with the "Anschluss." Hans told me that Wolf eventually wrote his memoirs from this time in a castle belonging to Prince Rohan and left them for safekeeping from the Nazis in Rome at the Vatican. Wilhelm Wolf died in 1939 in an automobile accident caused by his overtired chauffeur, on the way to see the Gauleiter in the Saarland where he had been ordered to appear.

Hans had a pleasant relationship with younger Catholics of the Hochland Circle in Vienna. He participated in evening discussions with clergymen about the Gospel of John. Later these ecumenical relationships earned him the curious black mark from the party people: They said he belonged to the "Catholic Action" but was also "a Niemöller man" in the Confessing Church. He became friends with the journalist Anton Böhm from the Hochland Circle. Hans saved him in 1941 from military service, where Anton really didn't belong, by bringing him to the Information Department of the Foreign Office in Berlin, where he himself was the assistant deputy.

Hans had a very disappointing experience through another member of the Hochland Circle in Vienna: Seyß-Inquart revealed himself to be a true National Socialist when the Anschluss occurred. He had himself appointed Interior Secretary in Vienna, but by May 1940 he was sent off to be the Reich Commissioner in the Netherlands. In 1946, after the war, he was convicted as a war criminal in Nuremburg.

Hans also soon made contact with artists, and not only with the members of the Viennese Secession; at their first opening exhibition, we unexpectedly purchased our first painting by E. Huber, and member Joseph Dobrowsky painted our two sons the next year. In January 1937 Hans wrote, "I have now secured the involvement of the Austrian artists in the grand opening exhibition of the 'Haus der deutschen Kunst' in Munich with the help of Gauleiter Wagner (!). For once, at least, a success . . ."

The cultural attaché was not only interested in the fine arts: music and film were also his domain, and we—Hans, and I as his companion—enjoyed going to concerts and exhibitions as part of official business, and even to the filming of a movie with Olga Tschechowa. We even took excursions together with the organist Franz Schütz and with Kabasta, whom we held in high regard as a conductor. I recall an excursion to Lunz Lake when the daffodils were blooming as especially nice.

However, not everything was enjoyable: "I have now taken over the cultural department," Hans wrote on November 24, 1935, and have immediately had a day of huge battles. Continual telephone calls with Berlin where the Ministry of Culture was at odds with Goebbels. But we remained firm, finally resolved the matter politically, and five minutes before the catastrophe Neurath [Foreign Secretary] personally obtained autonomous power for the Ministry of Culture. Everyone was flabbergasted and congratulated one another, but it is unfortunately much too early; that was only the first prelude of the fight that is before us. Prince Erbach [Ambassador] has been fantastic so far. Papen also accepted my report from yesterday. Hopefully—in the interest of the Reich—we will win the matter.

Hans had quickly recognized that the concert agent Mr. Beer was a cheat and was misappropriating money for which he was accountable to the cultural attaché, that is, to Hans. Since Mr. Beer was a "Golden P.C." [Party Comrade] with a party number under 10 and with personal access to Hitler, this fight was time-consuming and dangerous. On January 1, 1936, Hans wrote:

Remember that I wrote you that I had popped the boil— now the pus is flowing, but I fear that much more is coming. In any case, just as I expected, they have begun to shoot, and I had no choice other than to shoot as well. I haven't had to experience such a thing before, because up to now I have not had to fight so personally in the trenches. The most difficult part is putting broken people back together, people who have been frightened by threats and terror. One of them has collapsed with heart failure, heart spasms, after a truly unprecedented scene. The main thing is not to become frightened myself. You know that I am not naturally courageous. But I take comfort in the fact that there is a power that bestows strength to the weak, and that one can ask for that strength. Today was again a huge battle day of the highest degree.

January 19, 1936:

The work matter [Beer] that I recently wrote to you about seems today to have come to some sort of conclusion, at least of the first phase. A rather dubious personality has actually been fired. Unfortunately, there is still a terrible degree of disorder in the department. My predecessor only did the 'culture' part of the cultural policy; he skirted around the politics in a wide arc.

On October 17, 1936, Hans reported to me from Berlin:

Megerle told me today that concerning the request by Beer to expand his authority, the State Secretary directed: "Beer is unacceptable and has to be replaced by someone else." This turn came unexpectedly and the reaction of the office was equally surprising; Altenburg explained to Megerle: "Well now you have won, but Haeften will have to pay for it if you don't remove him from Vienna immediately!" Can you imagine this? The fury of Mr. Koderle [head of the Führer's Chancellery] towards me seems to be great indeed.

Luckily, Hans had true friends in the embassy: von Heinz and especially Gogo von Nostitz, with whom I remained faithful friends until his death in 1977.

After this debacle, Herr Beer threatened Legation Counselor Stein that he would actually take action against Hans if he didn't soon leave Vienna. So Hans could no longer travel to Berlin via

Prague and Dresden because a party friend of Beer's was the Gauleiter in Saxony, and one of his opponents had already disappeared into a concentration camp at the border crossing. From Vienna on January 7, 1937: "There was a great welcome when I arrived here. In the meantime, the news of my transfer to Bern came in! Everyone was flabbergasted at how I, already recalled once and transferred once, am here yet again 'until further notice.'" On January 11, 1937: "Still, the current attitude is further proof that they have no objection against me personally and only attack me in order to raise their prestige in Papen's eyes. So we'll just wait and continue working." February 2, 1937:

> When I was with Papen just now they brought him a letter from the Reich chancellery, a complaint against Nostitz and me, from Beer's corner. He immediately called for a secretary, dictated an introductory sentence, then let me dictate the rest—fortunately, I recalled the dates exactly. A truly prompt repudiation of the complaint. I thought again how this generous, resolute manner of Papen's pleasantly contrasts with the way the matter would probably have been handled by Stein [legation counselor].

Beer was then soon recalled from Vienna and even expelled from the party. Hans had previously received the following letter from Gauleiter Bohle, the liaison to the Nazi Party in the Foreign Office: "How can you, not a member of the party, dare attack a holder of the Golden Party Badge, whom we fully support?" Unfortunately, I can't quote the letter any further. Hans destroyed it in the fall of 1943 after he had kept it all that time "for afterwards." Now he believed this piece of writing, the only one saved, would arouse too much suspicion in case there was a house search, which was always a possibility.

During the Christmas holidays on the day of the "Innocent Children," December 28, 1936, Adda Benita was born in my parents' house in Dahlem. Hans registered her as "Benita von Haeften" at city hall in Berlin Zehlendorf, but in March 1937 she was baptized in Vienna as Adda Benita because my mother so strongly desired that her first granddaughter carry her name.

At the beginning of June 1937, we received the news that Father Haeften had suffered a stroke during a vacation with Mother Haeften in Cabarz in the Thuringian Forest. We rushed to the hospital in Gotha where, as Hans later wrote to Krimm,

> we remained at his death bed for several days until he gently gave up his soul. The majestic look of sublime and serene peace on his face after his death was beautiful. His facial expression was almost like a summary of the broad span of his life: from the Xanten Cathedral to the Weimar Classic, from the Prussian guard officer to member of the Leibniz Academy of Sciences—a noble balance and unity of faith and cosmopolitanism, discipline and love. I can imagine no more beautiful embodiment of the ideal of a Christian knight.

While South Tirol was not in Hans's Vienna operational area, during repeated vacations he had gotten to know it well and made friends with German nationals in the church, politics and economics. Such was the case with Canon Gamper (a German national representative in Trient) and Joseph Menz (a wealthy winemaker, fruit farmer, and forest owner near Meran), Franceschini, (a spice dealer in Bozen), and the businessman Walter Ammonn in Bozen. All these men were not fans of Hitler and thus did not fall prey to the illusory promise of "resettlement in Burgundy." They were so-called "long term residents" whose wives were no longer free to wear the Dirndl dress or the traditional "Gretchen" hair style. Conversations with these friends were fortifying on both sides, for instance in 1943 during Hans's recovery vacation (after our large bombing fire) when the Canon came from Florence for a secret visit. He had fled the Nazis and vanished into a convent after the October 21, 1939, treaty between Hitler and Mussolini dealing with the resettlement of South Tirol and the Upper Etschtal.

In November 1937 Hans was transferred from Vienna to Bucharest. "Leaving Vienna was and still is very painful," Hans wrote in December to Krimm. "We've fallen in love with the city, the mountains, and the people, and since our marriage we haven't felt so at home and comfortable as we did in our home on Glanzinggasse." He received a beautiful memento from the government: "a crutch cross made in gold, the knight's cross first class of the Austrian Order of Merit." It was confiscated after Hans's murder in 1944 with all his personal property.

On November 20, 1937, Hans began working in the German embassy in Bucharest. In the meantime, I had moved out of our apartment in Vienna and was waiting with the children at my parents' in Dahlem until Hans found accommodations for us. He wrote to me immediately: "What shall I say? Thousands of impressions, of course. In any case, it's not Europe. The Balkans? Hardly. Not clearly Asia either, perhaps more as I imagine Turkestan! Everything is completely different . . . just like in the colonies, with the charm of the exotic as well." He reported to Krimm on December 20, 1937:

> The city has no face at all; it has rather a grimace. It's a fantastic mixture of American style wooden houses, Boyar villas, Sicilian palaces, and warehouses. The people imitate Paris in the way they make themselves up, but look

otherwise rather Balkan Asian. In the circles in which we must move there is outrageous luxury: a normal breakfast consists of seven to eight courses, a variety of wines *and* champagne. Servants and chauffeurs, of course. Wealth and poverty are equally great here.

Hans's department covered "Culture and Minorities," so he had to initiate contact with churches, schools, universities, art and theater groups, the German-Romanian Society, and also with the local organization of the Reich Germans, even though he was the only non-party member in the embassy. As cover, I even had to join the National Socialist Women's League and visit the weekly knitting afternoons for Göring's air force, which, by the way, caused me to have to be de-Nazified after the war in order to obtain my pension. Of course, there were also many social duties inside the embassy, the German colony, and the diplomatic corps, which all stopped when the war began.

The Transylvanian-Saxon ethnic group interested Hans most of all. Surprisingly, the representative of this ethnic group and of this minority at the League of Nations in Geneva, district church curator Dr. Hans Otto Roth, visited him on the first day. A lively exchange with him began a political friendship. On December 20, 1937, Hans wrote to Krimm:

> My area of work is very interesting, but despairingly complicated and almost hopelessly bogged down. I got into a crazy situation right away—the election, in which the ethnic group has viciously torn itself apart. I fear that the result of the election will not contribute to unity, quite the opposite.

On November 22, 1937, he wrote to me:

Working with the boss will be very hard. He has very different fundamental views than we do in Vienna; for example, he would like the VDA [Association for German Culture Abroad] to be incorporated into the party organization because then his position with respect to the AO [International Organization of the Party] would be made easier. The ones who would be affected assure me, however, that the results would be disastrous.

And on December 2, 1937:

The boss is petty like a chancellor, wants to do everything himself, and floods the Foreign Office with paper. On the other hand, at my suggestion, he has now gone in a direction (concerning my section) that astonished the legation counselor with its boldness.

He wrote me again on December 15, 1937:

Today I am near despair. Crazy activity, meetings, invited out at noon, looking for an apartment and negotiations in between. Yesterday I was at a very nice performance of Fidelio at the local opera with German guest performers. Tomorrow Abendroth will direct the Viennese program! But the Viennese Orchestra is better! This morning for an hour I was with the archbishop, who showed me all around in such a friendly way that it was quite moving.

Earlier, on November 27, 1937, he had written:

Dearest Wife, finally a ray of hope! Today I took part in a weekend automobile trip by our economic association to Kronstadt and Hermannstadt. The Carpathian Mountains, which already had snow, were exquisite. Both cities are quite charming and have astonishing stores to shop for things one can't get in Bucharest. Nice old houses and places like at home. You will like this area—to Kronstadt a two-and-a-half-hour, to Hermannstadt a five-hour drive. The other trip very interesting, charming, the city Schäßburg, medieval like Rothenburg. On the way, many old castles and church fortresses. The people's dialect is somewhat like that of the Mosel area, where the 'Saxons' also come from; actually, they are Franks. The church costumes are truly wonderful, also the men's. A natural gas well that has been burning for two years, not far from Hermannstadt, is amazing—a powerful flame as tall as a skyscraper with a monstrous cloud formation over the countryside, fantastic at night. They cannot put it out. By the way, in Transylvania quite a large industry is built on natural gas; the gas comes ready to burn from the earth. Amazing richness. Very interesting also the large oil fields near Ploesti. We will visit one of these sites more extensively, at times the drillings go over 3000 meters deep.

Back after visiting us in Dahlem over the Christmas holidays, Hans was "immediately confronted with the Romanian winter: −26 C. degrees," and four days later: "Now there's suddenly been a thaw, all the streets have been transformed into lakes and swamps." In the neighborhood of the house that he rented for the first of February, "one can only use a row boat, there is no question of going for walks. They don't clean the streets here! Unbelievable. You should not push so much to come here; the help will leave us within a week." But the Sicilian style duplex had a roof garden "by today's standards enormous, surrounded by a sturdy high wall."

This became a marvelous play area for the children. The wonderful soirees we had expected, which Hans had repeatedly taught me to fear, did not transpire, mainly because the children and also Hans were quite often sick in Bucharest. It began right away with Jan getting scarlet fever; Dirk, Hans, and Adda caught it from him. As nurse, I was spared social duties for many long weeks.

On January 10, 1938, Hans wrote me: "There is once again a lot going on in my section, big operations are underway. Also, a horrible amount of paper work." In addition, the church struggle in Germany still kept him busy. He read in the press that "all Protestant pastors had now been let out of prison, with the exception of Niemöller, unfortunately. Hopefully, at least his trial will get underway!" The trial was soon held. Niemöller came out of the courthouse a free man but was immediately transported by the Gestapo to Sachsenhausen concentration camp as "Hitler's personal prisoner." Not until 1945 was he set free.

January 22, 1938, in a letter to me Hans wrote:

> . . . too bad that you are not yet here with me 'at the post,' but my trip [to Hermannstadt and Kronstadt] could not be postponed. I am just coming from a droshky ride with two jingling horses, for that is *the* means of transportation here; everything makes you think that you have been carried back to a small medieval town in the time of Goethe. It is charming here, just *too* bad—terribly bad—that you are not here *with* me. And also, quite apart from the fact that everything experienced together would really be much nicer, I miss you *very* much. Just like the time in South Tirol, at first it's mainly a matter of getting to know people, and you could have helped me so well with that! In the two days here so far I have seen a vast number of people, among them many of Ullmann's [Viennese friend, journalist, and

anti-Nazi] friends. In the city there is an endless amount to see, a beautiful Gothic church, old town fortifications and towers, the bishop's palace, charming spots, markets, old houses and courtyards, and a very important museum with the collections of Baron Bruckenthal, governor of Transylvania under Maria Theresa. . . . We have to look at all of that again in leisure. In addition, today at noon I received a bottle of wine from the Reverend Bishop [Friedrich Müller] from the church vineyards–absolutely fabulous!

In the surrounding area I've seen two wonderful villages: Michelsberg with a castle and a proud old church, charmingly placed, and Heltau, an extremely rich village with nothing but farmhouses, as magnificent as castles, and an impressive church fortress.

Tomorrow I will travel to 'Hohe Rinne,' 1500 meters high in the Carpathian Mountains, and the day after tomorrow to Kronstadt, where I will also visit Möckel. Tomorrow evening I've been invited to visit the director of the large diaspora home. . . . I have already met a great many people and have been asked about absolutely everything; the questions have not always been easy, especially not those about Rosenberg (head ideologue of the Nazis), who mightily upsets the people here and makes them nervous. If they just knew at home what havoc they are wreaking here, in a place where the all the ethnic Germans still belong to the church.

At the end of the trip, Hans visited Konrad Möckel in Kronstadt, pastor of the "Black Church":

I am still completely fulfilled with our long and fruitful conversation that both emotionally and intellectually satisfied me beyond all measure. A man who has more good judgment and insight into things in his little finger than everyone else taken together, especially those living in Hermannstadt. The latter are undoubtedly very intelligent, especially Müller and Buchalla. However, intelligence alone is apparently not enough to truly understand something; for that we just as much need the right disposition of the heart. And Möckel has both. I hope now very much to always remain in touch with him.

They began to offer one another true support. "Möckel is indeed the only person in this country with whom one can talk of matters other than diplomatic ones." Hans had Möckel's back when he opposed the dangerous plans of Bishop Glondy, who believed

to have now found the point at which he can incorporate the myth into Christian dogma, which signifies here the introduction of a "German Christian" era. If it comes, then naturally something like the "Confessing Church" will come. And then we'll have the whole quarrel here in the church, as well as between the church and the ethnic German leadership. Not just 800 years of history, but also the whole future would be destroyed over it!

Hans finally advised Möckel and Friedrich Müller to join the National Labor Front "because the decisions are no longer made in the consistory meetings but rather in the preliminary talks of the National Labor Front; with that the bishop is essentially deposed." To Krimm on February 2, 1938, Hans wrote:

It's simmering enormously here. . . . What an "episcopus," who doesn't know that a movement of the minds, such as the one that is emerging here, is never stopped by means of diplomacy, but rather can only be forced from spiritual power. And what does the Gustav Adolf Organization [GA] do? Which is supposed to be there to support the diaspora?! It continues to publish its magazine which could definitely be very useful. But how, when in the meantime the basis of its work goes to the devil in one gigantic mountain slide? . . . Why not work more directly, concretely, and a thousand times more effectively by going out and bringing the work of the GA closer to reality, making it more practical, that is, making it have to do with the tasks of caring for the soul and with churchly needs of the diaspora, going out, holding lectures, and above all, speaking to them confidentially in person, one after the other, hundreds of them, and bringing the important people—not only the bishop—to conferences in the Reich.

Next to matters of church policy, liturgical questions were equally interesting to Hans. So he accompanied and supported Möckel in his courageous endeavor: transforming the Sunday lecture activities given at the lectern into liturgical services before the altar. And fortunately, the congregation of the "Black Church" in Kronstadt went along with it.

The events in Vienna in the spring of 1938 distressed Hans greatly—he actually lay quite sick in bed. He and many Austrians had hoped for the union of Germany and Austria but had planned and imagined it quite differently than what followed on March 13th with the Anschluss. Although the German troops invaded without bloodshed, all the decisions were made in Berlin, and the Austrian Nazis were quickly driven out of all important positions by the Reich Nazis. Later, in Berlin, Austrian acquaintances came again and again trustingly to Hans as a "Non-Party Member" and complained to him of their disappointment and horror because they were not employed in Austria, as hoped, but rather were used for the most unpleasant duties in Poland or Holland or other conquered countries.

In the middle of March 1939, Hitler invaded Czechoslovakia and formed the protectorate of Bohemia-Moravia; further annexations were presumed. "Europe will be German to the Ural Mountains," our air attaché Gerstenberg often boasted after his first glass of wine, or he would say: "When the sleepy English wake up at nine o'clock in the morning, we'll have already sunk their fleet!" War seemed unavoidable.

"At first we spent the months and weeks here in unparalleled confusion," Hans wrote to Krimm on June 27, 1939:

Next to the actual work load that has swollen enormously, there was one festival after another: "Luna Bucurestilor" with the Busch circus and a huge firework display from Hamburg, including a bombing finale, military review, state youth day, sport day, a visit from Baldur von Schirach [Reich youth leader], Dr. Ley, a riding team with eight days of riding competitions and balls, visits from foreign states, an exhibition of "Joy and Work," car races, and so on. All of this, which often took up the entire day and night, was an "encore" to the usual work load. Now finally it *seems* that *somewhat* more peace and quiet has returned. Perhaps as a reaction to the confusion I have recently begun to do something very unusual for me—reading in an old Latin book and translating. It's a book that appeared around 1700, "Regia Via Crucis," written by a Haeftenus. He was provost of a reformed (!) Benedictine monastery—so you see that I am genetically ecclesiastically burdened. The book is written with enormous erudition and a plethora of quotations from the old Roman and Greek philosophers, and contains, next to some platitudes, also a number of beautiful thoughts and formulations. The Latin form of expression is beautiful. And Bible quotations are often easier to remember; for example, Hosea 13:10 "Ero mors tua, o mors," or: "Ego sum via, veritas et vita." But the most magnificent thing about the book is still the quotations from the church fathers. Incomprehensible that our church removed them from the family tree. Why? We are giving up a very rich legacy that is as Protestant as any kind of theology today.

In June 1939, I was able to take a carefree trip with the children to visit my parents in Mecklenburg, but Hans had to remain at work—in paralyzing heat alternating with

a fantastic storm, a drop in temperature of 30 degrees, a raging storm that simply broke the trees off and swept large stacks of hay like a pieces of paper over the steppe. Then, in addition to that, a downpour that sprayed completely horizontally over the ground, as though it had been forced out of 100,000 hoses with ten times the normal pressure. On the lake, ocean waves arose immediately with unbelievable foam crests, all the vessels broke free, and, unfortunately, six swimmers were drowned because they could no longer reach the beach against the terrible stream of waves, and their strength didn't hold out to reach the opposite shore. Attempts to save them, which I could observe, were hopeless because immediately after that an unbelievable hail storm began that made it impossible to see: hail stones larger than hazel nuts, that hit the roof tiles with such force that these broke apart in all directions. The roof held together relatively well at our place, but water came in everywhere in spite of the shutters, and it also rained into the bathroom through the roof carvings and into the hallway through the glass ceiling. The whole steppe around our house was one big lake. And then came the astonishing thing: the storm suddenly stopped and the sun broke through, and in a half hour everything was dried out and the streets bone dry! Today it is cloudy and pleasantly cool.

At the end of July 1939, Hans was able to visit us in Grammertin during his vacation and afterwards go with me to Tirol. On the return trip we took the Danube steamer for the first time from Vienna to Giurgiu—unfortunately not together, but still we all enjoyed the beautiful, interesting trip on the Danube. "It is too bad that I can't travel together with all of you," wrote Hans:

I had so looked forward to having the children for three days in peace. For how long you will then come, we don't know, of course. The [international] tension is extraordinary and naturally we indignantly rebuff the ideas coming from the English side concerning a conference (!). And Romania appears to gently drift off into the friendly arms of the Turks. Still, I believe that it will keep itself out of the game for some months. In any case, everything is unsure again, but this uncertainty is probably very beneficial for finding the right scale and getting our priorities straight again.

On September 1, 1939, the war broke out with Hitler's invasion of Poland.

On September 29, 1939, St. Michael's Day, Hans wrote to Krimm:

Dear Herbert, What times lie between today and your last letter from the end of July, and how the world has changed since then! Our brothers and brothers-in-law are in the army, and perhaps you are also already there, although not in a gray field jacket? Your task will be so much more difficult but also so much more urgent and necessary. It will take all of your inner strength to arm those fighting in the terribly hard and often horrible reality *verbis et opere* with "the shield of faith and the helmet of salvation and the sword of the spirit that is the word of God." May God be merciful to us and give us strength from the power of his strength so that fear of life and of death, when they come with their hellish doubts, may not shake us in the one certainty: "Speravi in Te: non confundar in aeternum" [In you I have hoped, Lord, I will never again be confused].

In September 1939, Wilhelm Wolf was killed in an accident. To Krimm, who had also known him, Hans quoted from one of Wolf's last letters: "We again hear the fighting angels like Grünewald, Albrecht Dürer, and Martin Luther rustling their wings, and full of distress hold our breath in the hope 'that our decisions are not made down here and that the empires of this world will be of God and his Christ.'" Hans wrote: "It would do all of us good if *more* remained to us from Wolf's life on earth than just his memory." He included much of his letter to Wolf's widow in the letter to Krimm:

As a politician he was truly μεγαλοψυχοσ: with a great soul and a great mind for planning and for action; he was never a slave to current tactics, though he handled them adroitly. Despite his sweeping perspective on the larger powers and forces of the day, he was nevertheless able to focus on the small and temporary details, always mindful of the purpose of all politics: to serve the growth of the kingdom of God in the world, to preserve the people through His sanctification.

Of course all letters were censored; I admire how Hans constantly sailed around the censors and was still able to convey the essentials.

He suffered more and more as a civil servant under the Nazi Reich. He spoke to me about it often and regretted not having immediately emigrated in 1933 as a Social Democrat, as did, for example, a son of the Reich court president Simon, a friend of his father's. On the other hand, he saw his place as being in Germany, although not, if possible, in a concentration camp.

In January 1940 Hans suffered a terrible accident. Full of enthusiasm he had gone with the children to slide on the iced-over lake near our house and had fallen with full force onto the back of his head. He remained unconscious for a good while and had a severe concussion. After several weeks, we were able to go to recuperate in the Kronstadt Mountains. There we enjoyed the magnificent outdoors and were able to hike and read. On March 1, our last day of vacation, Hans dictated to me a letter to Krimm:

I am now once again fairly well except for reading and writing which are still difficult. . . . We have often been at the Möckels. Being together with them did us much good, as you can imagine. Unfortunately, he has a difficult position. He is completely alone in the Transylvanian church, which drifts more and more towards corruption and dissolution.

In June Hans had to go to Berlin. They were already planning to call him back from Bucharest. The party people wanted to see all ethnic German matters in the hands of those who were "true to the party." And they most likely wanted to have him nearer under

Gestapo control. Jan was able to fly along with Hans to Berlin on this official trip—his first flight—and then travel for vacation to my parents in Grammertin, which was gradually becoming their main residence during the war. Dirk and little Adda soon followed them there with Fräulein Stengel. Hans came back from Berlin very depressed. He was outraged about the Germans' general enthusiasm over Hitler's victories and the defeat of France. Even Father Curtius enjoyed listening to the reports from the Wehrmacht—unbelievable!

At the beginning of August, Hans had to go back to Berlin. This time I went with him. After the paralyzing heat in Bucharest, I had a pleasant surprise during the evenings in the area of Hohen Tatra: I could once again breathe freely! Dörchen's due date was not far off. At first I remained with the children at my parents' in Grammertin. Hans often urged me, because of increased bombing attacks to escape to Vienna, Dresden, or even Bucharest. But even in those places it gradually became quite uncomfortable. So Dörchen was born in Berlin.

Right after returning to Bucharest, Hans wrote to me on August 8, 1940:

> The burgrave [Counsel General Rodde] from Kronstadt will now take over all the ethnic German matters and will come here every week, and the new man to be transferred here is supposed to function as his permanent representative and administrator; hopefully he'll come soon so that I can actually turn things over to him. I will temporarily retain cultural and other matters. My boss is of the opinion that things will be taken care of with this move, and I am to stay here. I am not so sure. . . . I actually feel out of place now, and I fear that there is nothing more I can do to further influence things; at most I could try for a

transfer to Pressburg. What do you think, and what does your father think?

On August 12, 1940, he wrote: "In the previous matters nothing new has come to my ears, so I am just waiting it out. By the way, I found out for sure that the most important issue is my friendship with Tiny [Martin Niemöller]. One just has to be patient."

Hans told me that Rodde, an SS man who was still sympathetic to Hans, reported to him confidentially which issues the Party held against him:

1. His father-in-law had been a "System Minister."
2. Hans was a Niemöller man and member of the Confessing Church.
3. He belonged to "Catholic Action."
4. He revealed that a Golden Party Member was a liar, which caused him to be expelled from the party.
5. Hans was the smartest in the embassy and therefore the most dangerous. So he had to be morally extinguished.

Hans objected that he had racially valuable children! He was actually quite happy with this "wanted poster," almost a little proud.

On August 18, 1940:

In the next days I will most likely be completely busy with working in the new gentlemen. A third of the work that I will hand over will be taken over by two consuls general, one legation secretary, one special representative, probably two typists and other personnel. There will be an extra shop set up in the building above the courtyard. I am happy now to be practically free of the work. There's still enough to do, especially because the boss wants to use me more for his own things, in addition to Stelzer. Whether we will remain or go somewhere else is still unclear. We must simply be patient.

In the meantime, Hans's brother lay wounded in Berlin. After receiving a letter from his mother, Hans wrote me on August 21, 1940: "It is not good that Werner had such a high temperature again and that the infected area is not improving. How does it help him that—as Uncle Walther [von Brauchitsch] wrote me—Sauerbruch [famous surgeon] was 'satisfied'? I think it's more important that the patient is satisfied. Having to lie still so terribly long weakens the poor guy more and more." Werner gradually regained his health and had to go to the front again in the north of Russia; we received upsetting letters from him there.

On August 26, 1940, Hans wrote me:

Everything is once again uncertain here. It's true we are in agreement with the Bulgarians, but it's not working at all with the Hungarians. . . . The third neighbor is cranking things up with Yugoslavia and apparently also with Turkey and is ordering more and more deployment in the East. So everything is uncertain. . . . We are very curious about the outcome from Vienna where the Hungarian-Romanian revision battle is now to be decided before the Eastern neighbor gets tied up in it! Hopefully, the solution will be fair to the proportional relationship of the population, which is, of course, quite overwhelmingly Romanian. By the way, the question of the resettlement of the Transylvanians and the Banat ethnic Germans is again on the agenda. You can imagine how worried we are about the decision. In the meantime, the Hungarians have now begun to bombard Romanian targets without inhibition. The Romanians defend themselves of course, and there have already been two air battles with one plane shot down. Curiously, it's exactly the same on the Eastern front. You can imagine how "uncertain" everything is here.

On August 30, 1940: "Today there is great unrest here: air combat with the Russians. Planes being shot down, border skirmishes. Furthermore, we are full of worry about Vienna, whether too much will have to be given up."

On September 1, 1940:

The decision about the transfer of two thirds of Transylvania caused deep shock and a landslide in public opinion with respect to us. Demonstrations against the transfer, speeches against us, and bashings of the 'Führer' are taking place; in Kronstadt, only 20 kilometers from the new Hungarian border, they stormed the German House; there are military personnel on the streets, and they dispersed a demonstration in front of the king's palace with tanks. Our embassy is now barricaded with troops for its protection. No one here expected this outcome. We have to expect that the government will collapse in the next two weeks. In this case we would take over the whole thing immediately; everything needed to do so stands ready.

But things turned out differently in Bucharest. On September 4, 1940, King Carol named Chief of the General Staff Antonescu the leader of the state. On September 6, King Carol had to completely abdicate in favor of his son Michael, and Antonescu ruled as a dictator. He aligned Romania with the Tripartite Pact and participated in Hitler's Eastern campaign starting in July 1941.

In September 1940 Hans was called back from Bucharest.

He was able to visit me in Berlin shortly after Dörchen's birth on September 14, 1940. At first, however, the goal of his transfer was not yet firm. So he asked me very skeptically if I would perhaps accompany him with the children to Moscow. This was simply not a question for me—of course we would have gone to Moscow with him immediately. But in the end it didn't come to that: Hans was transferred to Berlin as the acting director of the Information Department of the Foreign Office.

Now in October he had to manage our move since I had little Dörchen. Fortunately, we were able to stay in my parents' house in Dahlem, with all of our things, since my parents now lived mostly in Grammertin. We were very happy with that because we did not at all want to move into one of the many apartments from which the Nazis had recently driven Jewish families. In Bucharest Hans fortunately had help from Erzsi with "Schneidermann" and Hannes Brockhaus; Hilo Capesius also stood ready to help at his side; we had a warm friendship with her and Petris [pastor] for the whole Bucharest time and for always. Hannes Brockhaus belonged to a group of young men who had been sent for their military duty by the Abwehr into the Romanian economy and who were under Hans's protection inside the embassy. Hans had made it possible for Brockhaus to continue his medical studies in Bucharest on the side. Later, unfortunately, our connection to him was broken off, but my copy of a long letter from Hans dated January 1941 is preserved in which he answered Brockhaus in detail about his questions of faith. I'll only quote sections of the letter, but I think it can still be understood:

If I understand you properly, the question is perhaps as follows: does the human being need, in order to arrive at perfection, grace that has seized him from the outside, or is the highest good, the divine, immanent in his nature, so that in the course of his natural development he ascends to higher and higher forms of existence? Is the human being good by nature and does his good nature lead, by the strength of its own laws, its own drive, towards perfection, or is the human being evil by nature, succumbing to the earthly law of sin and death, a state out of which he is unable by himself to find a way out? . . . Christianity did not contradict the idealistic picture of the human being of antiquity per se, but it did extend it into two distinctive religious insights: the recognition of the diabolic . . . and the radical new perception of God as the God of merciful love, who in the form of Christ came into the greatly ruined world, broke through the hopeless circle of its law of decay and offered the human being, by calling him to follow, his supremely powerful divine help, so that even he, the human being, could break the stranglehold of satanic powers. . . . It's true that due to original sin the 'fallen man' of our earthly temporality has succumbed to the powers of evil, which are now stronger than he is . . . but even after his fall, the inextinguishable reminder of the original image remains, and also some of the divine germinal force, the power of the 'holy spirit.' . . . The remaining system is, however, threatened by atrophy and suffocation from opposing diabolic forces; out of this entanglement man cannot forcibly gain access to perfection, by means of his strength alone. . . . However, God's love mercifully reaches out to those who are incapable; he offers as help his grace. . . . It is not so that grace simply embraces those who are passively enduring. It is up to the human being to reach for the offered grace. And only he who struggles can grasp it, he who under mobilization of his last powers fights for his purification, he who opposes evil to his last drop of blood. . . . For that reason, grace is never merely a gift, but is also a task.

In October 1940 Hans became the acting director of the Information Department of the Foreign Office. Working himself in there took a lot out of him. But re-connecting with old friends, making new ones, and finding one's way, personally and practically, in the as yet unfamiliar war situation had all assumed greater importance. We quickly felt at home and on familiar ground now that we had our families nearby again, and that we were able to rejoin the Dahlem Confessional congregation where Dörchen could be baptized in the St. Annen Church. However, we missed Martin Niemöller; he had been incarcerated since 1937 in a concentration camp, and now the weekly prayer services were dedicated to numerous imprisoned pastors of both churches who were faithful to their confession. The list of imprisoned pastors continued to grow.

We were happy that Hans found Gogo von Nostitz again in the Foreign Office. He worked in the Policy I section, the military, but was soon transferred as consul to Geneva. He had fallen into disgrace with Ribbentrop; friends in the personnel department were able to protect him with this transfer. Adam von Trott, who had recently come to the Foreign Office, had been working in Hans's Information Department since the summer. Meeting again here was a joy for both men, and they remained good friends until death.

Through Nostitz and Trott, Hans was introduced to Peter Count Yorck in the winter of 1940–1941. During this time, the Circle of Friends, a group united by its opposition to Hitler, was getting started around him and Helmuth James Count von Moltke. It gradually grew and was later, during the persecution by the Gestapo, given the name "Kreisau Circle." Otto Heinrich von der Gablentz also belonged to it. Through him Hans reestablished contact with the Brothers of St. Michael in Berlin. It was a huge relief for Hans to finally have conversations with like-minded people and even eventually to make meaningful plans for the future—after "Day X," with no Hitler, which Moltke in his daily letters to his wife Freya called "the great solution." From May 15, 1941 on, Moltke again and again mentioned meetings with Haeften. That there was not an immediate mutual understanding between them was due to Hans's reserve and caution and his many years of experience in bureaucratic life: "Yesterday I easily pierced Haeften's hard shell. It takes a great effort to win over such people for the great solution because they know the routine too well. But if you are ever successful in breaking through, then you have a dependable companion—I mean Haeften." They met at various times, sometimes at Moltke's, sometimes at Yorck's, or at our house or at the Trotts' and occasionally also for supper or after supper at Yorck's place, which we could reach by bicycle in ten minutes. And Hans was even able to drive to the office with Adam Trott, usually in the little Fiat. We often met him and the Bielenbergs for Sunday walks in Dahlem with our children.

In spite of over-filled work days, Hans found time in May 1941 for a long letter to Krimm, who was still serving in Norway along with Theodor Steltzer in the army transport division. Both belonged to the Brothers of St. Michael and also had contact with Norwegian church people. Here are excerpts of the letter:

Your circle's conversation about the question of church influence on the world seems *very* important. You should continue it. Indeed, Lutheranism's (not Luther's) resigned acceptance, that the world is of the devil, has markedly contributed to the world actually becoming the devil's. When the church gives up on the world, the world becomes self-sufficient and obtains its values from itself. We know today what comes of that. I share your opinion that a church should have an effect by means of its presence. So it should not mingle in politics, that is, occupy itself with tasks belonging to worldly order. But the whole area of spiritual matters also belongs to the essence of the church, which includes pastoral care. If events or conditions that endanger the spiritual health of people now occur in the worldly order or disorder, if politics bring citizens into situations that they as Christians cannot be responsible for, then it comes to junctions and intersections of church and state. These are frequent and unavoidable because both institutions deal with the same people and because these people cannot or may not divide their own selves into citizen and Christian. When such overlapping occurs, which can be more or less critical, requiring decisions, or also more or less clear, the bishop's office of the church forbids the church "to be silent like a mute dog." The duty of pastoral care demands that the church speak, proclaim and warn. . . . If Christian peoples are taken over by the craze of political demons as they are today, then the voice of pastoral care in the church must also ring out publically and bear witness to the whole world. This also belongs to the essence of a church that is supposed to be effective in and of itself.

Yet there's more to the "Court Chaplain," I think, still more. . . . This applies in the same way to you theologically learned men who are Christians by profession, so to speak. If someone having to do with worldly order asks you for advice on how he should best solve some problem or another as a Christian, then you should know how to help him in a useful way. Practically speaking, if the question is posed more and more urgently these days about whether the development of state and society hasn't been, since perhaps the Renaissance, an evil false path, completely corresponding to the great decline into secularization which started then, whether we must not find a way out of the increasingly mechanized regimentation of human social forms since the beginnings of the territorial state to again make possible and cultivate natural social growth, whether we must not turn away from the exaggeration of the organizational principle towards an organic one, then homo politicus should be able to ask the theologian about the possibility of concrete application of Christian insights to the problems of human life (as applies to family and also to nations) in the here and now. In addition, the theologian, the sub specie fidei christianae, should also be able to give advice, not as a representative of the church, of course, for the church must deal with the unchanging certainties of faith, and not with changeable advice for the earthly order, which according to time and space and thousands of other circumstances of history must be varied. However, if not only the individual person, but also "the rulers and princedoms created by Him and for Him," if the earthly 'kingdom' also receives its ultimate direction from the eschatological sense of this word, if it is the highest goal of politics to serve the growth of the "coming" kingdom through just worldly order, to preserve and administer the affairs of the people in a way that they can become the closest to being "God's own people," then the Christian statesman should also be able to get advice from the men of the church for his tasks that are naturally not given to him by any task master other than the *one* Lord! . . . This what Augustinus meant when he spoke of the "civitas Dei": the overall structure of a uniform relatedness that extends from the here and now to what comes after, from earth to what is beyond. Catholicism has preserved this tradition more clearly, but has drawn what I consider to be the false conclusion of developing binding social state and society doctrines qua church forever, while the concretization of Christian faith in the worldly order remains a matter of worldly authority, and furthermore, must again and again take on other forms of order according to changing historical circumstances. Protestantism is freer in this respect, as is often the case, but it must finally become aware that it should be in the position to give answers whenever lay people ask theologians for their Christian advice about worldly matters.

In this letter Hans expressed thoughts that also played a role in the plans of the Kreisauers concerning a future state. Moltke hoped that the end of National Socialism would bring the opportunity needed to be able to rebuild in a trans-national way with new sovereign states.

In July I traveled with Jan, Dirk, and Adda to South Tirol to visit our friends the Menzes on Mount Vigilio, mainly in order to cure Dirk at mountain elevation (1700 meters) from repeated earaches and sore throats, which was actually successful. Hans gave me detailed reports while I was there about Dörchen, who was only ten months old and was still too small for a mountain vacation. On July 25, 1941, he wrote:

It is moving when after saying goodnight in the evening she stands up to see whether Jan isn't lying there in his bed. She also misses Dirk and Adda; she looks around her as though she is looking for the *little* people and can't figure out where they are. Perhaps I'll simply bundle her up in the sleeping car and bring her with me. Otherwise she is cheerful and in good spirits, frolics merrily as always and is conscientiously cared for by Erzsi. At the office there's a lot of work, but not much work gets done. All day today we had to debrief and interrogate Germans who were returning home from Russia [Hitler's attack on Russia had begun on June 22, 1941]. . . . Night, around 3:15 AM: Well, the air attack appears to be over. Since Dörchen had become upset down there, we laid her back in her little bed here upstairs. Erzsi maintained her calm and sunny disposition as always, although the unusual wailing of sirens was truly horrible. . . . I then took Dörchen and Erzsi away from the noise and light into the dark ping pong room and closed the door on the chatter. Then the sweet little creature actually continued to sleep. Unfortunately Mütt . . . was much more disturbing than the English planes. . . . Saturday morning: Dötte is very cheerful and at the moment is amusing herself with the little white bear. The sun is shining. Perhaps we'll have the opportunity today to go swimming with Trott at the Hundekehlensee. Next weekend Moltke has invited us to his estate in Silesia. I will abstain however because I can't take Saturday off.

So the relationship among the Friends was always strong. Adam Trott even came with Hans on vacation to South Tirol where we met each other at Zirmerhof. His wife Clarita had to stay home because she was expecting a child. Regarding a letter from Werner from July 15, 1941, Hans wrote:

They are marching day and night, but the Russians are masters of retreat and every few kilometers destroy the streets, to the right and left of which are swamplands. Then

Werner and others are sent out as small reconnaissance troops to find other ways to get through. But there are still almost always Russian units in these areas. The Russians also keep appearing in towns and districts that have long been reported as being free of the enemy—they are now fiercely fighting in these areas and enormously impeding our advance.

Some days later Werner again wrote about shocking hardships in heavy fighting, and Hans noted:

They march day and night and look like dead regiments when they stagger in—one could not call it anything else—their faces white with dust. Food supplies are causing the greatest difficulty. Vehicles have to be partially pulled by teams of men since there are fewer horses every day. They have now reached Narva at the Finnish Meerbusen; they are probably going in the direction of St. Petersburg. Unfortunately, Werner has a capital case of colitis with continual diarrhea, headache, and light-headedness. Since there is no special food at all, not even zwieback, and also no medications, he didn't eat for two days until finally he was so hungry that he ate some pea soup. We immediately sent him eldoform and charcoal tablets. God willing, by the end of the month he'll be doing better.

On August 6th Hans wrote: "Briefly, everything is fine with us. Dörchen is in the best of moods and in general very sweet. Yesterday she suddenly stood *next* to her stroller, squealing with laughter in the garden . . . Erzsi said, 'I just about died when I saw that.' Our little person thought Erzsi's reaction was so funny that she couldn't eat for half an hour because she couldn't stop laughing.

... Tiny [Martin Niemöller] has been brought to another hospital [Dachau concentration camp]. I will visit his family." Later we heard that he was imprisoned there in a cell with two Catholic priests, which helped him recover from depression and also gain back some weight.

On July 28 Hans, and my mother as well, went to see the internist Professor Siebeck for a thorough examination. According to Hans:

> he could only say that I am physically healthy and that under normal healthy living conditions my body would function normally. My physical capacity had its limits. I should eat a lot of fruits and vegetables, should exercise, and should not be at work from early until late with no rest in the afternoon. He thought Zinn's prescription was excellent: "do things that make you happy and take frequent vacations in the mountains." And everything would be better with general improvement in the condition of my nerves. But then there was, unfortunately, the sickness of our times. . . . Dörchen is—thank God—cheerful and very much disposed to getting the best of Erzsi, which Erzsi enjoys. . . . On Saturday I am invited to Schorsch [Maier], which I'm looking forward to.

So Hans still had contact to old and new friends and heard from all sides about the most appalling incidents in Hitler's crazy, murderous war in the East: right at the beginning of the war against Russia, the commissioner commanded that every imprisoned party functionary there should be shot immediately, hostages too; for example, for every three German soldiers attacked in Serbia, 1000 men and 240 women were killed. On August 26, 1941, Moltke wrote: "The news from the East is terrible again.

Apparently we have very great losses. That would be bearable if we were not carrying the weight of hecatombs of corpses on our shoulders. Again and again we hear that only 20 percent of transported prisoners arrive, that hunger dominates in prison camps, and that typhus and all other deficiency epidemics have broken out." Moltke again, on September 28, 1941: "Every day there are 6000 German and 15,000 Russian dead and wounded. . . . A terrible price must now be paid for the inaction and reluctance of the military leaders who had seen the need for Hitler's removal!" Also from on October 21, 1941:

> The day is so full of horrible news. What disturbs me most is the insufficient response by the military leaders; terrible new orders are given, and no one seems to see anything wrong with them. How can we bear the complicity? In Serbia two villages were burned to ashes. In one village in Greece 220 men were shot to death, and the village was burned down. In France extensive executions take place—while I am writing here. More than 1000 people are murdered every day, and again thousands of men become accustomed to murder. And all that is child's play in comparison to what is happening in Poland and Russia.

So the Friends, especially the ones working as civil servants of the Nazi state, had great doubts about whether they could remain in service. At home and elsewhere, they could not, and were not allowed to even mention the topic. Again and again people brushed off the news, saying, "Those are just tales of atrocities." Hans, in contrast to Moltke, whose letters to Freya I can now frequently refer to, never put anything in writing about these atrocities, and he also did not write about "the time afterwards," or "the great solution," as Moltke called it. For Hans, the Gestapo was always threateningly present, beginning already in 1933 and even more since Vienna.

On August 15, 1941, Hans put "Dörchen, with Erzsi, on the train to Grammertin. It is now time."

> Because today [August 13] it has now been a week that we've had air attack alarms every night. Last night what was apparently the hardest attack took place. Of course, we were in the cellar. Although Dörchen could not sleep for even a moment because of the shooting, it was touching to see how very well she behaved. Every once in a while she said something in a loud and clear tone in her baby language, but she never started crying. By the way, Dötte is so mobile that we can no longer leave her even in the playpen without tying it down; for otherwise she wanders so far with the playpen that she comes to the gravel, which she finds interesting. In Grammertin they'll be able to put her on the large lawn. She is now so cute and sweet that it's hard not to bring her with me.
>
> Wolfgang wrote most recently on July 30th; he is well, but always in front with the fighting troops in South Ukraine, now already almost to Dnjepr-Knie. Werner is near Narva in a swamp with mosquitoes and the difficult task of crossing the river, possible only in one place because of the marsh.

Yes, with our brothers in the war, we were able to meet Adam Trott for a wonderful vacation with the children in South Tirol. At Zirmerhof, high above the Etschtal with the view to the west towards Mendel, we had a marvelous time.

After these worry-free weeks in the mountains, as soon as

Hans returned to Berlin, he had to deal with the damage from a bombing raid the night before:

> There were a bunch of hits; on the way to the office I saw the damage in the Eden Hotel. Especially near Tempelhof Field a lot was ruined, also in five houses in Vreni's neighborhood. I called her and learned that in the future, they plan to take the baby to Alex at the hospital every night—in the long run probably not very feasible. . . . Vreni now hopes that you are going to Grammertin, so that at least one of the sisters is there; and you could also get along better with Mütt. This morning I called Grammertin and spoke to Klaus: Dörchen is doing well and plays with Stanzi [her cousin of the same age]. By the way, Vreni thought Dörchen has become Erzsi's child; Erzsi has taken her over completely and lets no one else go to her—which I think is very good with the chaos in Grammertin."

At the beginning of October, I came back to Berlin from South Tirol with the older children, and I soon went to see Dörchen and my parents. Jan now had go to school at Arndt Gymnasium. "The director was clear—even in the most serious of attack warnings, the school *will remain* open." Hans was very doubtful about whether Neustrelitz wasn't the better choice. However, it didn't come to that until 1943 after our large bombing fire. In Grammertin our three children got measles, which kept me there. Everyone got better, and Dörchen even learned to walk during that time.

On October 9th Hans wrote me: "The people here were again able to pour out their hearts to you, and that helped them for a while. Of course, the family is now broken up, but there's nothing we can do about it, and we must accept it as best we can. Anyway, most people today suffer even worse disruption. Jan is cheerful. He bought himself a relief image of the air forces of the world (except Germany), which he is proud of. He thought it was necessary to know what the others actually have, and for that he sacrificed 4.50." Already a year earlier he wanted a map "that shows all of England." Since with the colonies that was only possible on a map of the *world*, he thought that Hitler "must not have looked at the atlas before he began the war."

While I remained with the three smaller children until the beginning of December in Grammertin, Mother Haeften was, along with Erzsi, with Hans and Jan in Dahlem. Hans always told me what was happening, and it was touching to see how he took care of many family and household needs and did enjoyable Sunday activities with his loved ones, in addition to all his work and maintaining his connection to the Friends. For example, on November 26, 1941: "Earlier I went on a very nice bike tour with Jockel, then we drank a nice tea with Omelutti for the first Advent candle lighting. Erzsi's wreath made of your branches turned out very pretty. And now I've just come from an inspection of the cellar, at Jan's urging." They found "so many surprising things," not only withered dates and lard nibbled at by mice, but also "some nuts and hazel nuts for Christmas cookies" and three tins of sardines, so they "could enjoy one today. In addition, there are fortunately so many different things there that will certainly be welcome in the spring." Through his cousin Heinz von Brauchitsch he even got hold of, "a very fashionable Steirer jacket for Jockel, fourteen points from Dirk's clothing allowance card! And for Peter Curtius there was a tracksuit." Astonishingly, he also took care of the household help's needs from the various families: "I now have search operations running in Croatia, Hungary, Slovakia, Kärnten, maybe even in Alsace." Sometimes he could happily report about a beautiful concert by the Stross Quartet. On November 23, 1941, he used some days when he was home with the flu to write to Albrecht von Kessel:

> After three days of sleep and some contact with books, I feel inwardly, shall we say, a little better composed. In the meantime, they have indicated to me that I had better be healthy again by the day after tomorrow in order to be introduced as the newly installed connection man between the Propaganda Ministry and the Information Department of the Foreign Office to Reich Minister Goebbels. In addition, I hear that I have been made the personnel commissioner of the Information Department with the duty of implementing by year's end the departmental restructuring that was devised long ago. So with that I would have three jobs, each of which alone fills the work day. Under these conditions I am considering whether I should stay in bed or flee to visit Gogo in Geneva. . . . What you say about "outlasting" [from a poem by Stefan George]:

> > *'If we can but outlast*
> > *Every day ends with a victory'*

> is true, and we must force ourselves to do it. But it is a miserable activity when one experiences daily all the things that *do not* outlast, but vanish and are sacrificed, and when one can't help but live with the focus of existence actually someplace other than in daily outlasting. Do you know the Rilke lines which, to my surprise, I recently happened upon:

> > *I am like a flag surrounded by emptiness.*
> > *I sense the winds coming, and have to live through them*

While things below do not yet stir:
The doors still close softly and in the chimneys there is
silence,
The windows do not yet tremble and the dust lies heavy.
But already I know the storms and am as agitated as
the sea.
I spread myself out and fall into myself
And cast myself off and am completely alone
In the great storm.

At that time Rilke was alone with this "premonition"; today there are many who feel this way and so are not alone, but seen as a whole there are still very few, and they are lonely in the crowd. I think it's very nice and proper that you want to come here again in December to inspect your friends Καί ἐπιμελεῖδθαι τῶν Ψυχῶν [Greek: and to take care of souls]. According to Plato, that is *the* task of politics. Medieval society—in the Christian world view—thought the same. Our time will learn it again and will have to restore the toppled hierarchy of values. So make us happy soon!

Little Gabriel's baptism was at the end of October 1941. Hans wrote me: "I was also invited for afterwards, probably have to go, although I'm not at all in the mood for it. Yesterday had a very formidable experience that I will tell you about. Have great doubt about whether I can stay in this office." This was probably about the expulsion of Jews that began at that time. They locked Jews overnight in synagogues in order to transport them the next morning to Poland and to murder them there.

At the end of November 1941, Hans wrote to me about, among other things, the food supply situation that was becoming increasingly worse; he wasn't sure that I should come to Dahlem with Dirk, Adda, and Dörchen:

> Unfortunately, also no flour at all. I had one pound purchased in order to be able to send cookies to Werner in the field again, but that causes us difficulty with bread. We also received only one pound of oats, which we are saving for when someone is sick. There are almost no books anymore, all either out of stock or banned. Through Buchholz I was able to order Stifter's 'Nachsommer' for Alex, received, as a favor, a picture book that can't be torn for Dörchen, and ordered a Hungarian novel for Erzsi . . . In the meantime all sorts of things seem to be going on. Uncle Walter [General Field Marshall von Brauchitsch] has been removed, as well as his assistant. The person chosen to succeed him refused. So at the moment there's no one at headquarters. Yorck's boss has also been fired. . . . Please keep all this to yourself, at the most tell Father.

December 2, 1941: "Yesterday Brockhaus was here for supper and brought a large piece of bacon as a gift [from Romania]. He was quite affected by what he had heard during fourteen days of vacation at home—I was also deeply affected by his news. His younger brother was killed in action at Ilmensee. He found another brother in the military hospital in Ploest and saved him, with the help of his medical professor from Bucharest, from getting the wrong treatment due to a false diagnosis. He passed the Romanian yearly exam." News also came from his brothers in the East. Wolfgang was sent back from Ukraine: because his mother-in-law was born a Jew, even though she was baptized a Christian as a child, the German army could no longer tolerate Wolfgang! Letters came from Werner. He was happy about the cookies and letters, but as for reading a book, "Unfortunately, I come to that very seldom. I do manage to reflect, but usually I reflect 'about the well-being of the company' . . . nowadays that's way more than usual . . . infinitely many things to procure, which used to arrive through regular supply routes." Food provisioning functioned poorly:

Recently we succeeded in scaring up 600 kilograms of potatoes. Although they were charged against our account, we now have double what we had. And—the potatoes weren't frozen. . . . Unfortunately, I've recently had some losses. Then I have to write to the next of kin. But when someone is wounded, I also write; that's not usually done, but I think it's the right thing to do. A 16-year-old Russian girl just tried to defect. Some idiot or another shoots her just in front of our trench. I have her brought in, but she is critically injured and is going to die soon. We interrogated her. Things must be bad in Leningrad. Cannibalism is in full bloom. Also in the villages we occupy, people are dying by the dozens. Whoever dies, remains on the spot. Or is eaten up by the grieving family left behind. One of my non-commissioned officers recently found the remains of a child, from which the parents (!)—as it turns out—had sustained themselves for several days. You see, there are all kinds of things to make one reflective. I would like to read something by Stifter. Jean Paul's "On the Eternity of the Soul" is too difficult for me. I don't understand it. . . .

He reported that leading high-ranking officers went out of action one by one, or were being relieved:

If I stay here long enough, I'll become an army commander—where else will they find people? Regiments are now always led by majors. Your warm things are much too good for me. In spite of them, my nose is now causing me trouble. If my chap hadn't recently brought it to my attention that my nose had already turned completely white, so that I was able to quickly rub it with snow, I probably would have been rid of it. I occasionally read in your letter from March 1941 the part about "remaining patient." I can fortunately say that that is currently not at all difficult for me. However, I would really like to see you all now and again. So after a drink of your good tea, I will go check the trenches once more for the end of the day. Greetings and many thanks, Your faithful brother, Werner.

This was the last letter we received from him in the field. On February 2, 1942, he suffered a severe wound near Ilmensee in Russia—a shot through the groin and buttocks. A long ordeal in the military hospital. Afterwards, he was no longer able to serve in the field.

To further indicate the horrors and atrocities during the war, I'll quote from Moltke's "Letters to Freya." Hans knew these horrors as well; he told me about them many times. But nowhere did he write down the sorts of things as Moltke did on November 17, 1941: "Hunger, sickness and fear are spreading meanwhile under our rule. . . . Every day brings grim new glimpses into the depths to which people can sink. But in many respects we've already reached bottom: the insane asylums are slowly filling up with men, who during or after the executions that they should carry out, have broken down." On November 24th he wrote: "The war is looking very bad. In the East, Russian attacks on the whole front." Winter came, and caring for, feeding, supplying winter gear and accommodation were miserable. Things were also bad in Africa. More and more people knew about the expulsion of the Jews, and there was also significant unrest among the population due to the church struggle. Added to this was the attack in December by the Japanese on Pearl Harbor, the main base of the Pacific fleet in the USA, and with that Hitler's declaration of war against the United States on December 11th. Hitler's megalomania had no limits, and no one intervened.

Moltke worked with the Friends tirelessly on plans for the "New Order of the State" to become effective *after* the Hitler period, after the catastrophe that could not be avoided. In spite of a heavy load in the Foreign Office, Hans participated again and again in the conversations of the "Kreisauers." Moltke wrote Freya on January 10, 1942, "Yesterday I had a very satisfying conversation with Haeften. After things not at all going well for months, everything is now fine, and we have advanced to the point where we can communicate very quickly."

To convey Hans's basic ideas, which he certainly also put forth among his friends, I'll use selections from Anton Böhm's "Sketch," written in 1946 for Ricarda Huch. Böhm, employed in the Foreign Office in Hans's department starting in 1941, was a friend from the time in Vienna, and he lived with us after losing his apartment in a bombing raid in 1943. So he knew Hans very well. We frequently enjoyed his brilliant piano playing in the evenings—originally he had wanted to be a conductor. After the war, he became the chief editor of the "Rheinische Merkur."

As much as Haeften must have hated the Hitler regime, he loved Germany. Although he was brutally honest in his judgment of the national faults of Germans, although he often doubted in his darker hours whether the attempt to free these people should be made in order to protect them from complete disaster, his love for the German people, as well as his Christian conscience, caused him to revolt against Hitler. The influence on Western civilization of the intellectual and early imperial achievements of the Germans was always present within this highly educated man, who had the advantage over others with perhaps more extensive knowledge, in that his knowledge was truly and actively present. He recognized the obligation of the nation, emanating from its cultural and political history—he deplored the victory of Nazism among the Germans as a secular departure from the destiny of the nation. . . . He wanted to help liberate Germany. But he knew that removing Hitler and his whole political apparatus was only a beginning. What had to come next was even more difficult: to liberate the German people from their resentments, their illusions, their feelings of inferiority, on the one hand, and on the other hand, from their mixed claim to power—their false ideals of power and success. Liberating Germany further meant for him guiding it back to its true role in Europe and in the world: as a leading civilized nation, guarantor of peace, legally integrated into a European global community. And it meant something else for him, this above all: to make Germany Christian again. For Haeften and his circle viewed the turning away from Christianity as the true, historical-metaphysical reason for the impending catastrophe. This people, he believed, was particularly obliged to build a Christian ecumenism; that was the reason the Imperium Romanum was transmitted to the German people as the Sacrum Imperium. . . . But Haeften did not want to reawaken a "sense of a mission"; he was not a romantic. He knew that the Middle Ages, to which the Sacrum Imperium belonged as a political form, were gone for good. . . . According to his convictions, Christianity must be applicable, even in the political sphere, no longer in an institutional form, but as a realization of the Christian conscience. The requirement of the Christian statesman was now a just social order inside the country, and service to a peaceful order that binds nations internationally. A just social order was one of Haeften's main concerns. Haeften, who came from an old Lower Rhine family—he was not, as many think, an Old-Prussian squire—was a socialist. Not in the party sense. He had no party loyalty. In his view, the socialist order itself in the coming era was not at all in question. The parties only had to tackle and agree on the way, the methods, the pace and, in the border areas, the scale of the socialist reconstruction. It did not come to the development of specific details, but Haeften personally sought a cooperative form of socialism with extensive operational autonomy. He had a high opinion of the experience and the self-discipline of the German trade unions, in which he saw a mainstay of the future German state. At the same time, a special concern of Haeften's was preserving the personal freedom of individuals. He viewed personal freedom as being neither secured in the individualism and boundlessness of the early ideals of liberalism nor, of course, in complete bondage of ideological collectivism, but instead only in a permanently woven, continually renewed balance between individual rights and the demands of the common good. He used the term "personalism" for this order of balance; although not entirely adequate, it at least gave a name to what he meant. To give people the power of personal autonomy in the midst of the necessarily increasing planning and mechanization of the social being, he saw only one way: a new strengthening Christian religiosity, because Christianity is the religion of the personality, and the character of man as person in

Christianity reaches its highest value—as the image of the nature of God. Haeften's socialism was founded in ethical demands—the right of everyone to share in earthly goods is not set by law, but is rather an innate foundation of the natural moral order. Furthermore, socialism was for Haeften a natural consequence of democracy: the democratic categories of politics and the state would naturally expand into the realm of the economy and social structure. Democracy was for him a consequence of Christianity taken seriously, because of the infinite value of the individual soul and the equal destiny and the natural, personal rights of all people. He recognized democracy as a universal principle of the design of human coexistence. . . . Through practice it would come into its own. . . . For Germany, democracy also had to mean federalism, in addition to socialism. Germany should become a state—not a confederation!—strong enough in all matters concerning its own existence, but federally free in all the rest. For Austria, whose particular situation Haeften understood quite well, after the success of the overthrow of Hitler, a free referendum under international scrutiny was planned.

In foreign policy Haeften saw general peace as the ultimate goal. This corresponded to his irenic and ecumenical sentiments in religion. Utilitarian considerations could not make anyone a real, reliable, sincere friend of peace. . . . Within the 20 July group, which was not very homogeneous in its composition, the ideas on foreign policy had not yet been sufficiently clarified. However, for Haeften there was no doubt that Germany could neither opt for the East nor for the West; it had to take into account all the considerations of its geographical position in the middle and, above all, help win Russia for Europe, especially by finally offering it security against an attack from Europe through a friendly relationship with guarantees in place. . . . Haeften was well aware that all this demanded a long and difficult re-education, that it would not be enough to punish the war criminals.

This much from Anton Böhm's "Sketch" of Hans's ideas for a new Germany—after Hitler! Böhm stayed in touch with the Friends and also helped conceive and prepare the "Kreisau Papers."

Hans's infrequent letters contain nothing political, but they still tell us a lot about him. From a business trip in April / May 1942 with his colleague Voigt to Madrid and Barcelona, where they had to monitor a large company, he reported on the splendors of art, culinary pleasures, beautiful landscapes in the evening sun, a cold snap and the lack heating, his sadness that I was not on the trip, and of visits to colleagues and friends and of other invitations. On the way back they had the good fortune of being able to spend a few hours in the south of France: "In gorgeous weather we lay on the beach and enjoyed the beautiful Mediterranean Sea and watched the sailboats, and the seagulls that glided above us." From Geneva at Gogo's: "Spring is in full bloom in the gardens, even though it's still cold in the rooms. . . . Life here has an indescribably peaceful feel; it seems like an entirely different world, a permanent vacation." They devised a delightful plan for the summer: with the children, and for some of the time with Gogo, on the Riederalp in Valais. Because of a medical certificate, Hans was actually able to take this beautiful vacation in the mountains with excursions to the Aletsch Glacier and Eggishorn.

On April 25, 1942, Hans wrote to Krimm:

We are considering an indirect demarche for the purpose of your transfer to the diaspora area Romania-Transylvania.

Things are quite stirred up there. The regional church assembly has recently adopted a resolution according to which the freedom of the Gospel is henceforth limited by the requirement that it must not contradict the Germanic sense of justice and morality. Of course, the ethnic group leader decides whether a conflict exists. Möckel, who initially wanted to stay away from the meeting, has fortunately decided to attend—in this case it was quite necessary—and has publically protested there along with others. But he is now, just as the former Episcopal Vicar Friedrich Müller in Hermannstadt, almost under an imperial ban. He is really in a difficult position and could use help from friends. But it's very nice that his circle of brothers is growing, slowly but surely. This has encouraged him to continue on his way. After all, this is actually the building of a new foundation, under a hail storm of collapsing ruins.

In 1942 Krimm was working as a pastor for the Wehrmacht in a large military hospital on the front in Russia. "At least you can tell yourself that your work is infinitely more important than the stuff I wear myself out with here. . . . Making plans seems quite odd to us. The world situation is changing day by day. Now we understand the strict sense of the verse 'Your word is a lamp for our feet.' It illuminates only the next step for us, and we must be content with that." As an appropriate description of our world situation, he wrote Reinhold Schneider's sonnet for him—"Only Those Who Pray Can Overcome"—with its conclusion:

> *. . . Now is the time, when salvation is hidden,*
> *And human pride celebrates at the market,*
> *While people praying conceal themselves in the cathedral.*
> *Until God brings forth miracles out of our sacrifices*

And in the depths, that no eye unveils,
The dry wells fill with life.

At the end of May 1942, Pastor Hannes Schoenfeldt from Geneva went to Oslo by way of Berlin on a work-related trip. Hans knew him from meetings at Gogo Nostitz's. Hans informed him and Bonhoeffer, independently of one another, about the plans of the "Kreisauers" and their hopes for contacts with England before their meetings with Bishop Bell of Chichester. He was able to exchange the necessary information with Schoenfeldt during work conversations at the Foreign Office with Anton Böhm participating, while Hans conferred with Bonhoeffer only on unobserved walks before and after Bonhoeffer's Oslo trip. Shortly thereafter, Hans met on June 2, 1942, with Moltke, Steltzer, and Mierendorff at Peter Yorck's to pass on all the information.

In the next few days Eugen Gerstenmaier was informed, and Bishop Wurm was brought in through him. Hans and Gablentz informed Moltke on June 22nd, before his first conversation with Wurm. Wurm appeared ready to continue planning and preparing with the Friends. Everything appeared to be running satisfactorily.

Hans was unable to attend the meeting in Kreisau, although it's clear from Moltke's "Letters to Freya," Böhm's "Sketch," and the memoirs of Gerstenmaier, Siegmund Schultze, and von Hassell that he took part in and was actively involved in the discussions and planning of the Friends. He was interested in contact with the churches and most profoundly in the relationship between state and church, as well as in educational matters. His position as acting director of the Information Department was too exposed, and for years he had been under surveillance by the Gestapo, especially since his ultimately successful fight against the propaganda ministry in 1935-1936. But he said to me that if Adam went, he wouldn't have to, because they would always agree on everything.

In a long letter to Krimm, dated November 1942, Hans explained the statement of the Christian faith: not only

that God is the Lord of history, but also . . . that he realizes in history a plan of salvation, that he guides it to a goal of salvation, that he is building his kingdom at all times, even in this age, and is moving ever closer with each historical epoch towards final perfection. That rational thought is not able to see this salvation history, but instead perceives a horrible accumulation of calamities, nonsense and injustice in history, is probably due to the hiddenness of divine agency. It's hard to believe in salvation in the middle, below and behind the ostensible triumph of wickedness and violence in history. It is truly the case that "Reason fights against faith." A look at history, particularly the horrors of contemporary history, is a serious challenge to the belief in the omnipotence and mercy of the Lord. Luther once said that the images of godlessness, the oppressing pictures of sin, death and hell, "were there for no other purpose other than to fight them and cast them out." It's basically the story of Peter's walk on the water: when he looks at the water, at distress, danger and destruction, he begins to sink, and only when he sees the Lord can he grasp the saving hand. Both Dürer images preach that too: the one of the knight, who in the obedience to his faith goes his way without paying attention to the lurking figures of Death and the Devil, his view focused on the promised goal shown to him. And the picture of Michael fighting the dragon: with both arms grasping high up on the lance he performs the powerful, fatal blow. All power, all the transcendent weight of the moment is concentrated in the face of the conqueror. Luther described the imagination of Christ in the soul as the connection of the eye with that which is above!—very difficult to achieve, when imagination is repeatedly harassed by images of demonic terrors. Unfortunately, I am often wretchedly faithless and despondent, lapsing into the temptation of gloomy, brooding worry. How necessary is the daily plea: "help our unbelief."

At Christmas 1942, Hans wrote out for Krimm the deeply serious Christmas poem by Jochen Klepper and also had to inform him of Klepper's desperate suicide with his family: "His wife was Jewish and had a Jewish daughter from her first marriage, who was now supposed to be picked up: the mental anguish Jochen Klepper must have felt preceding this decision is unimaginable. And what an indictment of us in many ways, in that there is so little real community, so little Christian brotherhood, real pastoral care—God the most merciful forgive us and show mercy to the departed, that they may rest in peace and that his eternal light may shine upon them."

AT THE BEGINNING OF JANUARY 1943 THERE WAS A DREADFUL air attack in Dahlem where we lived. Our apartment was rendered uninhabitable due to a large fire from several incendiary bombs and a nearby aerial mine. The children were taken to friends in the neighborhood immediately after the air attack and the next morning to their Curtius grandparents in Grammertin. Hans, Jan, and I were invited by friendly neighbors (on Arnimallee) to live with them. But first we had to secure our belongings on Peter-Lenné-Straße and take care of the enormous amount of water left by the fire department. Soon we were able to find shelter in the Brauchitsch house, that is, the house belonging to Mother Haeften's brother, who was with his wife in Silesia. This was very helpful and agreeable to us, first of all because it was close to Jan's school, and secondly, because of the deep air raid shelter belonging to the Herr Field Marshall—you see, the air attacks were becoming more frequent. After the summer vacation, we put Jan in a different school in Neustrelitz. He was able to live with Dr. Hecker in Domjüch halfway to Grammertin, and Dirk later joined him there.

In the spring the congregation provided us with a parsonage to rent temporarily near our wrecked house. We lived there with Christel until January 1944. Then Hans moved back into the house on Peter-Lenné-Straße, where in the meantime the roof had been placed one story lower. During that time the air attacks increased, as did the damages and constant repairs, especially those necessary for the mandatory blackouts.

During the evening of the fire and afterwards, Hans had greatly overexerted himself and subsequently felt terrible. He was granted a vacation on March 15th and traveled with his mother to a sanatorium in Thuringia, which turned out to be a miserable experience. First he had to get over the flu, and then they relocated to a well-known little hotel in Cabarz on the edge of the Thuringian Forest. With the help of packages of groceries from Grammertin and from Werner, they were able to nourish themselves sufficiently and gradually become stronger, and when it wasn't too cold, they were even eventually able to do some relaxing reading.

On April 12, 1943, Hans wrote to Krimm:

The forest is so beautiful, the weather less so—snow-storms—and the inhabitants, as someone here said to me, "barbaric and weak spirited"! The churches visited by three little old people, the sermon very proper, but talking around everything that should be addressed; one has to say, even the Catholic church hasn't been able to deal with these heathens: In the book and stationary stores nothing but 'Germanic' things in a Wagnerian sense or

Barbara and Hans von Haeften in 1943
at the family estate Grammertin.

non-sense, enough to make a person seasick. But I wasn't, for I have a wonderful counterbalance: Stifter's *Witiko*, a wonderful book! And how relevant! A very strong sense of proportion, the balance between strength and gentleness emanates from it. It is a timely reflection on the Christian orientation of everything human, especially all public affairs . . . as much as worldly order is a matter of secular authority alone, it must still stand *together* in this connection with the spiritual life under God—and should certainly be informed by it. In the long run, the governed will only develop trust in the person who can say to them: "Do not fear, for I am under God" (Joseph to his brothers). Western civilization thrives only in the polarity, and the polar unity, of the state and the church.

Hans was not able to fully recuperate until May in the Martinsbrunn Sanatorium near Meran. I was even able to accompany him at first. We enjoyed a really restful vacation with beautiful walks and reading, and good, important conversations with our old friends from our Vienna days. Best of all, we found our special friend Canon Gamper in the same sanatorium. He could now dare to go back to his homeland from exile in Florence, for in South Tyrol the mood within German ethnic groups had relaxed somewhat and subsequently improved for our friends, the ones who stuck it out there. The Nazis felt disappointed by Hitler, even betrayed, for nothing came of his lunatic promise to resettle the South Tyroleans to Burgundy. Moreover, Hitler's murderous war in the East gradually opened the eyes of even the South Tyrol Nazis.

Hans returned from South Tyrol at Pentecost. We were now living with Jan in the parsonage on Drygalski Straße. On June 15th Hans returned to his office. The last meeting of the Friends had taken place in Kreisau from June 12–14; right afterwards on the 16th Hans met with Trott and Gerstenmaier at Moltke's place. They gave reports and talked about the days in Kreisau and then about the continuing program for the summer. Moltke wrote in a letter to Freya: "A general sense of satisfaction prevailed, especially with Haeften, who was favorably impressed."

Now and again I had to go to the children in Grammertin, even though in the meantime we had obtained Fräulein Stengel to help. She even gave lessons to Dirk and Adda there. Our friends from Bucharest had not forgotten us, and so Hans could report to me enthusiastically about glorious gift parcels: bacon and oil and soap; and a mammoth case of kitchen items came from 'August the Delectable' [August Westen]. "Jan really sweated when they had to unpack everything in the garden because, of course, the gigantic crate wouldn't go into the house at all. And August calls that 'a few kitchen items.'"

After the summer vacation, Jan stayed in Mecklenburg, and I was mainly with Hans and Christel in Dahlem. "How long this will be possible," Hans wrote to Krimm on August 12, 1943, "we simply don't know. The city awaits heavy air raids by night and day in the near future, with the goal of eliminating Berlin. The prevailing mood is similar to the one described in the Bergengruen novel about the expectation of apocalypse." Gradually the air attacks became quite uncomfortable, and so when the alarm was sounded we often went by bicycle to the Brauchitsch bunker and after the all-clear went quickly back to do any necessary repairs or even put out fires from incendiary bombs.

In addition to his regular involvement with the Lutheran Church and his ecumenical connections to the Roman Catholic Church, Hans had maintained good contact with the orthodox church of Romania since Bucharest. In conversations with Professor Nicifor Crainic he gained a clear picture of theological and church policy questions. And the book by S. Boulgakoff *Les Religions de l'Orthdoxie* was so important to him that he wanted to translate it from French into German; unfortunately, he had no time to do that. Now, as the acting director of the Information Department, he had to go on a work-related trip to the Balkans in the fall of 1943. He flew via Vienna, Athens, and Sofia to Bucharest to gather essential information from the orthodox churches of the Balkans. In October he wrote me a letter from Saloniki. He had been involuntarily detained there because suddenly an officer who was "particularly important to the war effort" needed the seat on the flight that had been reserved for Hans. Nevertheless, he was a guest of the consul general and was well taken care of, and he had some free time for a relaxed vacation letter: "I am very satisfied with Athens from a work point of view. In between work business there was still time for a trip to Eleusis and for a visit to the Acropolis, during which Professor Walter, director of the earlier Austrian Archaeology Institute, was kind enough to give us a tour. That was not only quite interesting, it was also very enjoyable. Especially the Parthenon! I kept thinking how much you would have enjoyed it, the exquisite forms and lines and proportions and not least the colors. After the war we must simply go again." From Bucharest Hans went for a short time to visit our friends in Transylvania. I am placing Konrad Möckel's "Remembrance of Hans Bernd von Haeften" at the end of my narrative.

After this business trip, Hans composed a detailed memorandum for the Foreign Office: "Questions of German Policy Concerning Balkan Orthodoxy." I recall that he really had to rack his brains to make his findings and suggestions palatable to the party people. He called for a reorientation of German policy towards orthodoxy in the subjugated and confederated countries of Southern Europe. A positive attitude toward Balkan orthodoxy would be necessary, especially in the course of the realignment of

Europe. "The ecumenical tendencies of the Balkan churches must be promoted, and the Reich must be ready to gradually take over the role of political protector of Balkan orthodox Ecumenism."— "If Germany misses this opportunity, there is the danger that it will fall into Russia's lap."—"If a new German policy concerning Balkan orthodoxy is to be successful, this purely external and highly sensitive complex must be shielded from disturbances from the area of domestic German church policy at all costs, that is to say, from the struggle between church and state."

Life in Berlin in the fall became increasingly hard. The bombing attacks became more frequent and severe as the nights grew longer. Two bombed out colleagues of Hans's, Anton Böhm and Alexander Werth, now lived with us in "our parsonage." Moltke had also been bombed out and now lived with the Yorcks. More and more of the city was destroyed by fires and high explosive bombs. Public transportation functioned intermittently, or was often completely cancelled; one rode a bicycle whenever possible. Telephone connections often didn't go through, and calls out of the country were soon completely forbidden.

On December 11th I had to leave Dahlem due to phlebitis. Ulrike was on the way, and life in Berlin had become too strenuous and too unsettling. Fortunately, I was able to travel with my brother Klaus to Grammertin, and at my parents' home things were good for me and the children. Hans was able to be with us and relax over Christmas until January 2nd. He enjoyed the rural peace and the children. They took him to their own proper Christmas celebration in the forest: "the most beautiful Christmas of his life."

At the beginning of January, Hans's sister's house, in which his brother Werner and his mother also lived, was transformed into a heap of rubble by a direct hit. Luckily, Liet had already evacuated to the country with the children and her mother. "Werner laughed himself to death when he came home at ten in the evening and could no longer find the house; the entryway had disappeared without a trace," so he went by bicycle to Hans. There was a wild effort to save a lot of things from the rubble, including all kinds of provisions from the cellar. Liet and Werner were able to live temporarily in the Brauchitsch house. Later, Werner and Mother's Fräulein Clara moved in with Hans, who was now living again in the Curtius house; it was a floor lower but was weather-tight. The move was very troublesome for Hans, along with his work and the many unsettling bombing raids, whose blazes often dangerously lit up the sky over a wide area. "In light of the uncertainty of our household management, Böhm and Werth have now decided to move in with Six, where there's a girl who can cook very well. That's actually a good solution for when Fräulein Clara comes." All of the household business was problematic and difficult for Hans, but a half year later these hardships were forgotten in light of what happened to us. And after the war we were simply thankful for everything that had remained with and in the house.

Moltke was arrested on January 19, 1944. At first, the only thing that incriminated him was the fact that he had warned Kiep of his impending arrest; not until July 20th was his connection to the Friends known. Although I see nothing in Hans's letters about it, it's clear that the circle of Friends had lost its center and its driving force.

At the end of January, Werner suddenly saw an opportunity to kill Hitler. When Werner was with Hans and went to get his pistol out of the suitcase, Hans demanded of him: "Is this really your duty before God and our forefathers?" Werner capitulated. Hans was, however, very troubled that he had intervened since Nazi crimes and bestial war atrocities continued.

At the end of February, Hans was promoted to legation counselor first class with the title of "privy counselor" in the Foreign Office. At the same time, along with this promotion through the

Reich Chancellery, Hans's rejection for membership to the Nazi Party arrived from the Party Chancellery—both documents had Hitler's signature. "By the way," he wrote, "when Six communicated the matter to me, the truly friendly applause I received made me happy" [Letter from March 3rd]. During this time Hans was much stressed; he often had to represent Six as the acting department director. The air attacks were now occurring frequently, even during the day. "The work load is insane," he wrote on March 16th.

Hans received sick leave on April 23rd and went to a health resort in Karlsbad for four weeks. His mother followed him there. Shortly before Ulrike's birth he visited me in Neustrelitz and was able to accompany me the next night to the clinic for the delivery. The next morning, May 19th, he greeted Ulrike and me joyfully, and soon thereafter he brought Jan from school to join us.

We did not remain in Neustrelitz long because even there it was dangerous due to low-level air attacks. Hans spent a few undisturbed, peaceful, sunny days with us in Grammertin. He was now declared 'available' at the Foreign Office and was waiting for his transfer, which was still uncertain. So he was able to visit us now and again and escape the air attacks in Berlin. And he could also distance himself from weighty considerations and practical preparations for the assassination attempt and overthrow that he was constantly confronted with through his brother Werner, who had become Stauffenberg's adjutant in the meantime.

All of this caused us to plan Ulrike's baptism right away. That was the last happy family celebration in Grammertin, on June 25, 1944.

Hans was with us again on July 19th for Jan's birthday, and he was able to take an unforgettable walk with the four older children, who were on school vacation, to a neighboring lake. But Hans was already in a state of great anxiety on this day, July 19th, and he passed it on to me. He expected his brother Werner's call at any moment. The date for the assassination attempt had been postponed twice because one of the "leaders" was missing. "This time, the film must roll," Hans said to me. Even if Göring or Himmler should not be there, this time the alarm of the Berlin guard could not be called back—it would have been too noticeable and would have aroused suspicion. Anyway, Hans suspected that the assassination plan had already been discovered. Above all, he was full of doubt as to whether it could even succeed. "The curse of 'too late' has long been lying over the whole thing." He often said to me, "If murder of a tyrant is allowed at all, then during his rise to power! They should have acted before Stalingrad" [1942-1943].

I must add that he did not necessarily believe that Hitler had to be murdered. He much preferred for Hitler to be judged by a court. (Gerrit von Haeften, Hans's cousin in the Foreign Office, was able to confirm this for me in 1970.) In spite of this, Hans finally agreed to the assassination attempt. I am certain that in spite of its failure, he would never have been able to decide otherwise, even though he believed the commandment "Thou shalt not kill" was completely binding, and he considered himself guilty due to his consent. He felt that he and the other Friends were mainly to blame for not having summoned enough imagination to find a political solution that could have caused Hitler to fall and bring about a coup. However, now they could no longer wait it out and watch all the injustice. Now they had to act, even with violence, before the Friends of the resistance all individually disappeared without a sound in prisons and concentration camps. Bonhoeffer had already been arrested in 1943 and Moltke in 1944; Elisabeth von Thadden and Kiep were murdered by Hitler's myrmidons. Mierendorff had been killed in an air raid. Now Leber and Reichwein had fallen into a trap, and the conspiracy would soon be discovered. However, from an international point of view, even a successful coup wouldn't bring much. "Now it's only a matter of an orderly capitulation," Hans said to me on July 20th. And so he went, not at all happy or even sure of victory, into the decisive battle, when he left us on the morning of July 20th, riding his bicycle to Altstrelitz for the train to Berlin.

That evening I heard from a radio report that an assassination attempt had failed! "The Führer is alive . . . a military putsch." I did not listen to the radio in general as I knew too well that every statement was a lie, and yet, the "failure" was correct. I did not dare telephone Dahlem until the next afternoon. There I found out from Jankofsky, our custodian, that Hans was greatly worried about Werner because Werner had not returned home last night. I knew that this was already the news of his death.

I know from a detailed report by Wilhelm Melchers how the hours on July 20th in the Foreign Office went by for Hans, along with Adam Trott and the Friends that were brought there, Melchers and Alex Werth. Hans himself did not tell me about it in as detailed a way when he returned to us, just for the night of the 21st, very agitated and deathly pale. He wanted to tell me about Werner's death and to say good-bye to all of us—and to explicitly give me his last farewell. Hans was very dejected and filled with worry about whether he could withstand the interrogations without giving away the Friends and our good cause. I was strangely calm; perhaps this was a comfort to him—even though when I later sat in my cell in deep despair and distress, it seemed almost harsh. But on this morning of leave taking it was amazing that I was able to comfort him with the promise Christ made to his disciples: "When they now will give you over, do not worry how or what you should answer. For what you should say will be given to you in the hour of need. For it is not you who are speaking, but rather the spirit of your Father, who is speaking through you" (Matthew 10:19).

And that's how it was. Hans stepped before Freisler at the People's Court with self-confidence. The photos of a press photographer and the documentary films show this clearly. I quote

Hans von Haeften at the People's Court on the day of his execution, August 15, 1944.

the wording of the debate between Hans and Freisler according to Dr. Jens Peter Michael's article "Hans Bernd von Haeften" in the *Deutscher Juristenschrift* from December 1995:

Hans von Haeften, August 15, 1944.

On August 15, 1944, during the proceedings against Bern-
hard Klamroth and others, Hans Bernd von Haeften was
also interrogated. A section from the official film recording
documents this [F=Freisler, H=von Haeften]:

F: What was your last position in the Foreign Office?
H: Legation Counselor.
F: Legation Counselor. At the end you were active, you were
    Acting ... Director of the Cultural Policy Department.
H: Yes.

F: Now then. Don't you realize that when a people is strug-
gling hard and when one of the probably thousands of
colonels that there are in the army of this people has such
an opinion, it's treason to deviate in any way from loyalty
to the Führer . . . ?

H: I no longer felt this duty to loyalty.

F: Aha, so, then it's clear that you didn't feel it, and you said
to yourself, if I don't feel loyalty, I can commit treason.

H: No, it's not exactly like that, but rather I thought . . . that is,
according to the view I have about the historic role of the
Führer, namely, that he is a great executor of evil, I was of
the opinion . . .

F: Well then, now it's quite clear. There's nothing more that
can be said about it.

H: That's right.

F: A fine civil servant in the Foreign Office. So then I'll ask
another question: And you dared to be an official in the
Foreign Office?

H: Yes.

F: So. It's not worth wasting any more words on this topic. I
think any additional questions would only diminish my
impression.

Freisler abruptly broke off the interrogation. Later the head state
prosecutor Lautz went back to this unbelievable incident from
the trial proceedings in his last address to the court. He said: "In
two points my impression of the proceedings today contained
something unusual that I would like to place at the forefront of
my address . . . The second point is that one of the accused dared,
dared after the monstrous extent of his guilt had been emphati-
cally placed before his heart by the chief presiding judge, this
accused dared to give an explanation that dwarfs everything else

we've heard in this area concerning his opinion of the Führer and the people. None of all the accused who have been interrogated dared such an explanation; he dared to do this, even though in the meantime he would have become conscious of the fact that he, with his act, had become the executor of everything evil. I mean the accused, von Haeften." Freisler wrote briefly in his judgment explanation: "His hate-filled words spoken before us demonstrate the way he [von Haeften] thinks—that he sees in the Führer the 'great executor of evil.'"

Eugen Gerstenmaier later said that Hans Bernd von Haeften's statement had actually been the decisive testimony of the whole resistance.

According to the death certificate from April 15, 1948, "Hans Bernd von Haeften died on August 15, 1944 at 20:15. The cause of death: hanging." That is, he died on the day of the proceeding and pronouncement of the judgment at the People's Court.

After the proceeding Hans was able to write his farewell letter to me. However, I didn't receive it until February 5, 1945. I received the death certificate in April 1948 and only by asking for it because of my widow's pension.

Hans's Farewell Letter

My dear, dearest wife, my good Barbara,

Most likely in a few hours, I will fall into God's hands. There-fore, I want to take leave of you. Briefly, a few practical matters. My will is in the small suitcase in Dohnenstieg. Give the gold watch to Jan, the other (in the little blue bag) to Dirk, one pair of the cuff links (gold or mother-of-pearl) to Johann Robert. Remember the provisions; a portion perhaps to Mutti and Liet.—I would be happy if first Father and then Klaus assumed the guardianship. For spiritual questions, seek Herbert's council. All the godparents will also help you. Tell Jan, as our oldest, that I ask him to help you in every way, especially to work hard in school and to cheerfully obey you. In raising the children, remember music (singing!), the fine arts, hiking in the beauty of nature; all this will guide their senses towards higher and nobler things and to pure joys.

Bärbel, have the children memorize many Bible passages and songs so that they may carry them in their hearts in times of hard-ship. There will be periods of doubt and distance, but life will bring the children back to a solid foundation, *if* it is laid in their youth. Christus est via veritas et vita.

Should the children want to get engaged one day, remember

that, if needed, a parental "no" can prevent harm. Hopefully, that won't be necessary. For the inscription on your or our tombstone, I would find our wedding vow fitting ("God is love. Whoever lives in love lives in God, and God in him." 1. John 4:16) and added to that the words, "So, whether we live or die, we belong to the Lord." (Romans14:8).

Photo-Rabe on Klopstockstr. 3 below the dentist still has a passport photo of me. If it turned out well, you can have copies made.

Barbara, during these weeks of imprisonment I have quietly submitted to God's judgment and recognized my "unrecognized misdeed," and confessed it before Him. "To hold God's commandments and practice love and be humble before your God:" That is the rule I have broken. I did not hold sacred the fifth Commandment (although I once pulled Werner back with it) and I did not take seriously enough the commandment "to be silent and abide." Above all, I did not practice love toward all of you who were entrusted to me. For your sakes, for Mutti's and our parents' sakes, I should have stepped away from everything. Please tell them—along with my deepest thanks for all their help and love—that I ask them with all my heart to forgive me. Bärbel, I did all of this with the conviction and the intention of doing right before God. In truth, I was disobedient, although I honestly implored Him to guide me on His paths, so that I would not lose my footing; yet I did lose it. Why? Amidst all the doubts, I may not have waited quietly and patiently enough for Him to reveal His will to me unequivocally. But perhaps all this has been His unfathomable, holy and benign decree.

My dearest wife, I die in the certainty of divine forgiveness, mercy, and eternal salvation; and with devout confidence that God, in his boundless mercy, will transform all the misery, pain, grief, distress and desolation that I have brought onto you, and which tears my heart apart, into blessing, and that His fatherly hands will lead you all on your earthly paths and finally draw you to Him. The Lord in His mercy will gradually soothe your pain, soften your sorrow, and still your suffering. Your love will stay the same for "it never ends."

My good Barbara, I thank you from the bottom of my heart for all the love and all the blessings that you have given me in the fourteen years of our marriage. Please forgive me any lack of love. I love you far more dearly than I have shown you. But we have an eternity ahead of us to show our love for one another. May this thought be a consolation to you during the sadness of your widowed years. I am certain—may you be too—that the two of us will be reunited with all who are dear to us in God's ineffable peace (which is at once the most perfect rest and the most blissful movement in the service of God), in adoration and the immediate experience of divine love, in the wondrous shelter of the Savior's mercy and kindness, in the redeemed bliss of being God's children. Even now on earth you belong to the body of Christ; this union is experienced most deeply in the Sacrament of the altar, in the presence of the Lord, who unites all of His followers in miraculous ways—be they on this side or the other of the great transformation.

Pray the 126th Psalm for me; the last sermon that I heard in our village church on the day of my arrest, was about this psalm. And with this pray Psalm 103, give praise and thanks.

My last thought, beloved wife, will be that I entrust you, my dear ones, to the mercy of our Savior, and my spirit into His hands. Thus I will die *rejoicing* in faith. And I wish, my dear Bärbel, that you, too, may remain "the ever-cheerful Frau von Haeften." Have fun and laugh with our children, cuddle and be merry with them; they need your joyful nature; and know that nothing could be *more* in keeping with my wishes.

So I greet you my dear dearest ones with the old greeting

"Rejoice! Rejoice in the Lord always and I will say it again: rejoice! And the peace of God will guard your hearts and your minds in Jesus Christ."

Greet and kiss our dear children from me, dear Jannemann, good Dirkus, loyal Addalein, precious Dörchen, and sweet Ulrikchen. As for yourself, my dear, most dear wife, my good, most beloved Barbara, you I kiss and embrace and hold in my heart with the deepest, most imploring wishes for time and eternity!

Your Hannis

Adam sends you greetings. Keep your friendship with Liet and Clarita and Marion.

Give Mutti a copy of this letter. I hope still to be able to write to her.

In 1946 I received through Clarita von Trott the important pictures of Hans before the People's Court, given by a press photographer to Mrs. Leber and identified with the help of Poelchau. Among them was the special picture of Hans after the hearing.

In 1947 a comforting message in the form of a letter from our aunt Gustel Kehl reached me. During an air raid in August 1944 she had been sitting in a bunker next to an officer she didn't know. He told her, without being aware of our relationship, that he had to be present as a witness at the execution of the men of July 20th, on August 15th. He said that he was deeply impressed by the attitude—or rather, the bearing—that two of these men had in dying, and he said their names: von Haeften and Klamroth.

A Remembrance of Hans Bernd von Haeften by Konrad Möckel

Recorded in 1946 or 1947 for Ricarda Huch

I NO LONGER REMEMBER EXACTLY WHEN IT WAS THAT THE young German diplomat visited me in Kronstadt for the first time. [On January 14, 1938]. But I do know that already on his first visit, he made the greatest impression on me of all the many Germans we met here in these turbulent years. It may have been the end of 1937 or the beginning of 1938. He brought me greetings from a mutual friend, of whom I am very fond, and that made us open with each other, right from the start. Even at that time, we Christians had a certain reserve towards visits that represented official Germany. But with Hans Bernd von Haeften, there was from the very beginning a deep understanding, you could say even a warm friendship. I have never seen a man who combined such deep and generous love for people and for God with such legal and diplomatic talent. As Transylvanian Saxons, we were often disappointed that Germans from the Reich, often quite educated people, could manage to show very little understanding for our character, our fate, our joys and sorrows. With von Haeften it was different. He understood our soul and our destiny better than we did. He was our good angel in the too short period of his service in Romania; he diverted calamity from us as we were forced ever deeper into the Nazi terror, often endangering his own position.

I will never forget the impressions that I have of him from occasional visits to his home in Bucharest. The tenderness and love that von Haeften surrounded his wife and children with. The innermost vitality and soulfulness of each word that was exchanged there, all while he was under enormous stress due to a huge workload and was carrying a great responsibility—the then young man held the position of legation counselor. When he came for lunch after strenuous and unsettling hours at work, he was pale and drawn, and it took a while for his disciplined and loving spirit to completely vanquish his physical exhaustion. When I, on one of the darkest days of my life—I was waiting to deal with difficult travel requirements for permission to go to Berlin to bury my eldest 19-year old son—had to spend hours in the expedition office of the embassy in Bucharest, I noticed how the name of Herr von Haeften was mentioned over and over. All significant matters were dealt with by him. Not because he took them on himself out of ambition, but because he towered over the rest due to his expertise and reliability.

But much more unforgettable were the visits from the von Haeften family in Kronstadt and the walks we took in the beautiful surroundings. Here in the rejuvenating relaxation of those vacation days, the full expanse of his heart and mind showed itself. During these walks, in many conversations, we discussed the fate of our people, of the world and related questions of time and eternity. Then the suffering he experienced as a dutiful German who had to serve the Hitler regime broke through with poignant, but also amazingly mastered humanity. He saw through the madness of this system, and its destructive danger to humanity, all the way into its last spiritual depths, and yet was bound by sacred duty to it. Was it not the perfect right of every good, decent German during that time to sit in a concentration camp? How much longer could he bear the hypocrisy? We watched this difficult internal struggle with admiration; he made the decision to go the hard way, to enter into active service each day, fighting for reason, justice, fairness and humanity, even though that appeared to be a losing battle. When the war broke out, this difficult emotional stress increased substantially, but it also caused our friendship to become that much more intimate. It was so comforting for both of us that a friend was nearby, whom we could completely trust and with whom we were so completely in tune. Von Haeften was then removed from his position by the machinations of the party people, mainly by our ethnic group leaders in Kronstadt, and we were then only able to maintain our connection through correspondence, which was very meaningful and intimate, but unfortunately also difficult and sparse.

The deepest and strongest bond of our friendship was that von Haeften's thoughts and feelings were rooted completely in the Christian message. Above all, he was able to see, with rare clarity and detail, the relationship between the spiritual life of the Church and the great historical events that beset us. What he had to say about current events as a Christian had a prophetic force. I will let him speak himself from some passages in his letters.

Berlin, November 4, 1940 (After a presentation of our Transylvanian-Saxon, ethnic and religious/church situation)

"LET THE FORE FIELD THAT CAN BE SECULARIZED GO, BUT ON the actual, spiritual battlefield you must resist without regard to the devastation. The facade of the 800-year-old building will crumble no matter what. Lay the foundation for the future building, without concern for the ruins collapsing around you; although it will be a ridiculously small stone, it is the start of a cathedral. This is the mission of your circle, even if it should all melt down into one point."

Berlin, March 19, 1941

"THE MERE RESTORATION OF YOUR CHURCH FORTRESSES MAY have value for museums and history . . . but what everything actually depends on is the completely new construction of the fortified church: the Church as a 'mighty fortress.' Of course, the position you will have there will be difficult, for mentally and spiritually you are in the old Transylvanian situation again: on a lonely, forward outpost. But basically we are all on a lost outpost: it is the common fate of Christianity in the world—today more than ever. What a wonderful assurance to know that just this lost little band is the least lost."

Berlin, June 14, 1942 (In view of the church-political
struggle in our Lutheran Saxon church)

"IN THE LONG TERM, THE INEVITABLE STRUGGLE CAN ONLY BE based upon the true spiritual foundation that your circle of friends has been striving for. We are very pleased to hear that the work is thriving. We must keep in mind that one day when the great disaster comes—and it will inevitably come—all other foundations, except for this one, will collapse."

"WRITTEN EXCHANGE OF VIEWS IS ALMOST IMPOSSIBLE. Instead, the community of worshipers, through which we feel constantly connected to both of you, is becoming an increasingly supportive certainty. As our Christmas wish I am you sending a poem by Jochen Klepper."

Haeften lived entirely in the evolving Christian Church, which can solely provide the way to help our nation and the world. I have met no theologian or lay person so far in my life who could have seen the distress and task of our Lutheran Church in a similarly unsentimental and clear way, but at the same time with all the fervor of a loving heart; and who with this heart and his farsighted spirit lived in the new time and, with that, in the new form of a spiritually alive Church. He knew about the *Church* that will become the fate of the world.

We saw each other one last time when Hans von Haeften came for a short stay in Transylvania in late autumn 1943. He gave us a great preview of the political developments that have come to pass, up to the last details. In opposition to all foolish hopes and biased fears, he had a sweeping assessment of the historical events, which, in fact, have materialized in their monstrous enormity. His great concern at that time was, as in the past, that when the terrible collapse and the great mass of misery arrived, a sheltering power would allow the people to salvage something, and that they, in time, would begin to prepare and to cultivate this last refuge from despair. However, this last refuge—that was quite clear—could only be the faithful Christian community. At the time, Hans von Haeften said in view of our Transylvanian-Saxon fate, contrary to all rose-colored and all darkly pessimistic expectations, which could be heard everywhere, that all of our life here would be destroyed, except for whatever held to the church. Hans Bernd von Haeften went like a shining star through the little life that we led in this corner of the world. However, it was not a cold, distant light, but a very close one, that illuminated and warmed with a very unusual love. What he was to us obliges us to love in the most powerful way and to believe and not lose heart. One part of the great sacred duty that the entire German nation has to its martyrs has also come to us in a very special way, through our encounter with Hans Bernd von Haeften.

Signed, Dr. Konrad Möckel, Lutheran Pastor in Kronstadt.

Ricarda Huch, *In einem Gedenkbuch zu sammeln . . . :*
Bilder deutscher Widerstandskämpfer, ed. Wolfgang M. Schwiedrzik
(Leipzig: Leipziger Uni-Verlag, 1997).